CONCILIUM

THEOLOGY IN THE AGE OF RENEWAL

CONCILIUM

CONCILIUM/VOL. 38

CANON LAW

THE SACRAMENTS
IN THEOLOGY
AND CANON LAW

edited by ✠ NEOPHYTOS EDELBY
TEODORO JIMÉNEZ-URRESTI
PETRUS HUIZING, S.J.

VOLUME 38

CONCILIUM
theology in the age of renewal

PAULIST PRESS
NEW YORK, N.Y. / GLEN ROCK, N.J.

PAULIST PRESS
EXECUTIVE OFFICES: 304 W. 58th Street, New York, N.Y., and 21 Harris-
    town Road, Glen Rock, N.J.
Publisher: John A. Carr, C.S.P.
General Manager: Alvin A. Illig, C.S.P.
Asst. General Manager: Thomas E. Comber, C.S.P.

EDITORIAL OFFICES: 304 W. 58th Street, New York, N.Y.
Editor: Kevin A. Lynch, C.S.P.
Managing Editor: Urban P. Intondi

Printed and bound in the United States of America by
Wickersham Printing Co., Lancaster, Pa.

CONTENTS

PREFACE

✠ Neophytos Edelby/*Alep, Syria*
Teodoro Jiménez-Urresti/*Bilbao, Spain*
Petrus Huizing, S.J./*Nijmegen, Netherlands*

"The admirable sacrament of the whole Church", in the words of the *Constitution on the Sacred Liturgy,* implies a double aspect of this "complex reality"—that of its inner, invisible life, and that of its outer, visible life—which both signifies and brings about its inner reality.

The inner reality can be looked at on three levels: the Church is the sacrament of "intimate union with God", "a people made one with the unity of the Father and the Son and the Holy Spirit", since God is one and three-in-one; she is the "visible sacrament of . . . saving unity" in Christ; she is also the sacrament "of unity for the whole human race". These definitions are all to be found in early paragraphs of the *Constitution on the Church.*

This triple—trinitarian-Christian-human—aspect of inner life and unity is seen to be both signified and caused in the visible aspect of the Church, the "sacrament of unity, the holy people united and ordered under the bishops".

The aspect of outer, visible reality can also be studied on different levels: the level of the exteriorized and thus subjectivized life of Christians; that of objective features established by immediate divine law and fulfilled in Scripture and tradition for faith, in the sacraments for sanctification, and in the hierarchical constitution of the Church for her social structuring and gov-

1

ernment; and that of objective features established by ecclesiastical law, which provides a more definite shape to the features established by divine law and gives rise to the formulation of "symbols" and "dogmas" in relation to faith, to the detailed configuration of the sacramental signs, and to canonical discipline, or "canons", with reference to the actual carrying-out of life in the hierarchical communion.

The sacramentality of the whole Church is expressed in a special way in its sign-causes, the divinely instituted sacraments. In them, the supernatural trinitarian-Christian life of the Church is expressed and produced in a particularly intense way. In them, too, the visible social life of the Church is also expressed more intensely, since they are *sacramenta fidei*, divine, institutionalized means of sanctification and communion. In themselves, they sum up the whole Church.

This explains the very special emphasis which the Church places on the ecclesiastical objectivity or positiveness given to the sacraments in and by Canon Law. This means, on the one hand, that this positiveness must not run counter to the nature of divine law as expressed in the sacraments, which belong to the deposit of revelation and tradition; and, on the other, that she must be careful to adapt herself to pastoral requirements, since the sacraments were instituted as means of salvation and so must form an integral part of pastoral care.

This volume of *Concilium*, in the desire to bring out all these aspects as accurately as possible, proposes some reflections based on the doctrinal content of the sacraments, on what is "of faith" in them, which may contribute to the making of pastoral decisions in the light of today's requirements and so open themselves to all possible facets of positivization—that is, of Canon Law. García Barbarena opens with a general view of the relevant bases of canonical ordering of the sacraments. Then, since the field of the canonical aspects of the sacraments is so wide, we have concentrated on particular points: the rights of the baptized person (Ter Reegen); the minister (Mostaza Rodríguez) and the age (Ruffini) for confirmation, the indissolubility of matrimony (Huizing), and the case of interfaith marriages (Örsy). The sacrament of orders receives fuller attention: the unity of the priesthood expressed in concelebration (Falsini); the unity of the universal mission fulfilled in the multiplicity of canonical missions (Jiménez-Urresti); pastoral communion on an international scale as evidenced in the supranational episcopal conferences (Klostermann); the unity of the local Church in the bishop (Corecco). Finally, there are some observations on the life of the presbyter (Gastgeber) and the deacon (Hornef) in the light of the present requirements of the sacramental ministry.

Some of these reflections and observations are clearly debatable. Each writer is responsible for his own views, expressed in the hope of helping both the reader and the development of Canon Law with fidelity to the basic theological imperatives and the directives and rulings of the magisterium.

PART I
ARTICLES

Tomás Garcia Barberena/*Salamanca, Spain*

The Canonical Ordering of the Sacraments

I

SACRAMENTS AND STRUCTURE

In the ecclesiology of the manuals, the sacraments are means given by God to the Church for the sanctification of man, vehicles or channels of sanctifying grace, each with the form appropriate to its particular character. The Codex, faithfully following this conception of them, considers the sacraments as *praecipua sanctificationis et salutis media* (c. 732, § 1) and classifies them among the *res* which are *media ad Ecclesiae finem consequendum* (c. 726). They therefore appear in Book III, *De Rebus*.

This conception seems to assume that God at a given moment established the Church as a visible and hierarchically ordered society, and that later seven means of sanctification were placed at the disposal of this ready-made Church, and these are what we call the sacraments. Now this understanding of the sacraments is not that of Vatican Council II, and one might even call it erroneous, because the sacraments are part of the essential, inner structure of the Church, and are precisely what gives the Church her outer, visible character—that is, her juridical character.

The theological bases of this understanding of the Church are the incarnation, Christ as the primary sacrament of salvation, the Church herself as "the universal sacrament of salvation" (*Con-*

6

stitution on the Church, n. 48), and the sacraments as concrete embodiments of the Church.[1]

The sacraments are not only seven channels of grace, but are at the same time seven juridical acts which define the position of the Christian in the Church. Article 11 of the *Constitution on the Church* explains this for each one of the sacraments: baptism makes him a member of the Church with the obligation of confessing the faith he has received; confirmation binds him more closely to the Church and increases his obligation to defend and propagate his faith—it must be received before he can marry or take orders (cc. 1021,§2 and 993,§1) and some would maintain that it should precede the eucharist. The eucharist is participation in the Church's greatest social act: it is both a sacramental institution and a juridical one, since participation in the eucharist is the juridical realization of the unity of the Church, as is stated in n. 2 of the *Decree on Ecumenism*.

This is why excommunication means above all exclusion from the eucharistic communion, and the prohibition to participate *in sacris* with non-Catholics (c. 1258) refers principally to the sacramental aspect, and particularly the eucharist, the sign of unity.

On the subject of penance, the *Decree on the Ministry and Life of Priests* (n. 5) says that through it "sinners are reconciled to God and the Church, the reconciliation with the Church being a sign and cause of reconciliation with God. The anointing of the sick likewise binds the sick person to the Church in a special

---

[1] There is an abundant bibliography on the subject matter of this article. I am principally indebted to the following works: K. Rahner, *The Church and the Sacraments* (London and New York, 1965); P. Smulders, "The Church as the Sacrament of Salvation," in Barauna (ed.), *The Church of Vatican II* (not yet published in English; French and Spanish versions are available); *idem*, "Sacramenta et Ecclesia" in *Periodica* 48 (1959) pp. 3-55; E. Schillebeeckx, *Christ, the Sacrament of the Encounter with God* (London and New York, 1963); M. Useros Carretero, *Sacramenta Ecclesiae et Statuta Ecclesiae en la Eclesiologia de Santo Tomas* (Rome, 1962); R. Schulte, "Kirche und Kult," in *Mysterium Kirche* II (Salzburg, 1962), pp. 714ff.; St. Thomas Aquinas, in IV sent. dist. 17 & 18 and *Summa* II-II, 39, 3, and various well-known treatises of sacramental Canon Law.

way; his attitude should be one of obedience to and confidence in God so as to bear with illness and death, and his attitude to the Church should be of one who is dying with Christ who bore death", while "the whole Church commends those who are ill to the suffering and glorified Lord, asking that he may lighten their suffering and save them" (*Constitution on the Church*, n. 11).

The juridical aspect of matrimony is so clear that there is no need to describe it here, and the same goes for the sacrament of orders which places the ordained person in the clergy with the power of orders and the possibility of exercising jurisdictional powers, thereby establishing the principal, divinely originated, division of the members of the Church into clergy and laity (cc. 107 and 548).

Taking their stand on patristic and Scholastic teaching, modern theologians attribute a sacramental structure to the Church. A sacrament is not something that the Church holds as a deposit, but something that belongs to her very being and that makes the Church present every time it is produced. The Church is visible, external and juridical through her sacramental nature, and, as St. Thomas says, all law in the Church is based (*consistit*) on the sacraments; it is either sacramental of itself or can be reduced to what is sacramental, and, in the final analysis, to the eucharist, "the center and summit of the sacraments" (*Decree on the Church's Missionary Activity*).

The juridical consequences deriving from this approach are extremely important. In this article I just want to make some observations on its application to the sacramental structure of the Church and her constitutional law.

Modern writers have a very high opinion of the teaching of St. Thomas, who affirmed on various occasions that the Church was "fabricated", "founded", "built" and "instituted" by faith and the sacraments of faith. Vatican Council II affirmed that the Church should be regarded as a "visible structure" in which are to be found juridical agencies and the mystical body of Christ (*Constitution on the Church*, n. 8).

The same ingredients and the same problem of unity are to be found in the sacraments, which are also external and visible signs with the divine and invisible gift of grace hidden in them. This likeness indicates that Church and sacrament are really the same thing: the Church the proto-sacrament and the seven sacraments so many more actualizations and realizations of the Church making contact with individuals to offer them the life of God in the lives of each one of them. In Christ the divine and the human are unconfused but inseparable, because the hypostatic union is everlasting; so, too, in the Church are the hierarchical society and her power of saving, and also sign and grace in the sacraments.

Since 1940, the works of Carnelutti and Fedele have reanimated the discussion from the canonical point of view; yet, though fruitful, we have the impression today of having failed to get to the root of the problem owing to our defective ecclesiology. The characteristics of canonical ordering and its differences from secular law were sought in the *different ends* of the Church and secular society. The method is not illegitimate, but the "why" of things does not always explain their "what". Canon Law is not the same sort of thing as secular law, but only analogous to it, because of its sacramental character.

The juridical constitution of the Church is in fact an expression of its sacramentality. The Church is visible and hierarchical *through* the sacraments. I shall examine later how the hierarchy stems from the sacraments; here I want to show that the external visibility of the Church is that of the sacraments. Neither the Church nor the sacraments are the juxtaposition of two elements, one visible (the sign) and the other invisible (grace). The reason the Church is visible is not that she *has* some visible elements. The formal visibility of the Church consists in the fact that her mystery is made apparent in her organization, in her hierarchical and juridical relations, because everything in the Church—people, things, structures—is informed by a supernatural principle that effects an interior transformation. Without this inner supernaturalization, the people, things and structures would not form a Church, nor would the Church be formally visible with a visibility that would distinguish her from other purely human societies. From all this it follows that constitutional law in the Church is not limited to "hierarchology"; the basic norms of the sacraments belong to the sphere of the Church's law and should be incorporated in her revised Codex, if it is finally decided to proceed with one.

II

SACRAMENTS AND THE LITURGY

The canons dealing with liturgical celebration are also to be found in Book III of the Codex, *De Rebus*. The rules laid down in them are generally superficial and concerned with detail. Now the liturgical aspect is an important zone of coincidence between the sacraments and the Church, since both are institutions of worship. As Schillebeeckx writes: "A sacrament is the manifestation of the divine love that Christ feels for men [the gift of grace] and of the human love that he feels for God [worship]." The *Constitution on the Sacred Liturgy* (n. 59) affirms that the sacraments are acts of worship, modern theologians regard the Church as a worshiping society, and Vatican Council II fully endorsed this point of view (*Constitution on the Sacred Liturgy*, n. 59; cf. nn. 7, 10 and 99, as well as the *Constitution on the Church*, n. 10), even though it made a careful distinction between the hierarchical priesthood and the common priesthood of all believers. The theological bases are the same as those noted in the previous section. Everything stems from the incarnation, since Christ is a priest because he is man and precisely in virtue of the hypostatic union. "In Christ there came forth the perfect satisfaction needed for our reconciliation, and we received the means for giving worthy worship to God" (*Constitution on the Sacred Liturgy*, n. 5). The priesthood of Christ is present in the Church as in an organically structured unity which "through

Christ offers worship to the eternal Father", and so "in the liturgy full public worship is performed by the mystical body of Jesus Christ, that is, by the head and its members" (*Constitution on the Sacred Liturgy*, n. 7).

What is the link between the liturgical aspect and that of sanctification by grace common to the Church as proto-sacrament and the sacraments as manifestations of the Church? The sacraments sanctify through being acts of Christ and acts of the Church. They are not a form of magic; they are external signs that are valid only if, in the bosom of the Church, they are impregnated with the faith and merits of Christ. This way they fit into the Church is described by the term *res et sacramentum*, an intermediary element between the outward sign and the sanctifying gift of grace, since it is *signifying* in relation to grace and *signified* in relation to the outward sign.

The water of baptism, for example, is first an outward sign bringing juridical membership in the Church, a membership that both signifies and produces the grace of baptism. Smulders has traced the parallelism between these three trilogies of concepts: law-worship-spirit; outward sign-character-grace; juridical society-worshiping society-society of grace. In this systematic construction the liturgy of the Church and the sacraments form the intermediary element—*res et sacramentum*—linking the extreme elements of sign and grace, law and charism. It consists in the character in the three sacraments that stamp it on and in the equivalent or *ornatus* entity in the other sacraments.

Here I want to consider only the fact that the liturgical aspect is inseparable from the sacramental and ecclesial reality, and the liturgy is the same as that performed by Christ the priest on the cross, his priesthood perpetuated in the Church in time. The Church is a worshiping society with a sacramental structure; thus the basic norms of the liturgy must be in the fundamental code of the Church, with the primacy given to eucharistic worship.

But the Codex does not mention the priesthood of all the faithful or their active priestly role in the liturgy; they are only granted the right of receiving spiritual goods and aids to salvation from the clergy (c. 682). Vatican Council II took a different approach, calling the Church a priestly community with a sacred nature and an organic structure, and affirming that this community is brought into operation by the sacraments (*Constitution on the Church*, n. 11). The *Decree on the Apostolate of the Laity* says that the laity are "consecrated into a royal priesthood and a holy people" and that they have an active part to play in the life of the Church as sharers in the threefold office of Christ —priest, king and prophet.

The present Codex does not treat the sacraments as liturgical actions either, not even the eucharist; it seems rather to exclude them from the concept of liturgy, since c. 1256 defines liturgical acts as "instituted by the Church". Instead it abounds in minutely detailed rulings that would better be left to individual bishops. It is to be hoped that the new Codex will base the ordering of the liturgy on the principles of the *Constitution on the Sacred Liturg*y and emphasize the sacramental basis of Christian liturgy. The ecumenical demands of worship in common with other Christians (*Decree on Ecumenism*, nn. 8 and 13) will also have to be borne in mind, particularly common worship with the Eastern Churches, which, "though separated, possess true sacraments" (*Decree on Ecumenism*, n. 15).

III
SACRAMENTS AND THE HIERARCHY

The Church is not made up of the sum of two elements, one juridical (legislative, judicial and coactive power) and the other supernatural (the power of orders and of the magisterium). Any exclusively temporal power in the Church is an unacceptable hypothesis on any grounds. The power of the Church must be supernatural and visible at the same time. Therefore, in the hierarchy all power is raised to the supernatural order: subjects, authority, juridical relationships and the ends of hierarchical action and of all canonical ordering. One must beware of certain juridical formalisms which have been introduced too definitely in Canon Law as they have in civil law.

Basically, the hierarchy is unique (cc. 108, §3 and 109). Ordination and ordination alone is what introduces a man to it and enables him to receive a canonical mission. The history of the concept of hierarchy would show that the present distinctions between orders and jurisdiction stem from the dislocation into autonomous powers of what were originally acts of one sole power. There are not some "king" hierarchs sharing the kingship of Christ and other "priest" hierarchs sharing in his priesthood. The bishop, by virtue of being a bishop, directs the regular and fruitful distribution of the sacraments by his authority (*Constitution on the Church*, n. 26); his authority is exercised "in the name of Christ" and is "proper, ordinary and immediate" (*Constitution on the Church*, n. 27) so that, represented by the presbyter, he is in a certain sense present in every local assembly (*Decree on the Ministry and Life of Priests*, n. 5).

Orders does not of itself include the power of jurisdiction, but this is rooted in orders without which it would have no *raison d'être*. Orders is the immediate cause of what St. Thomas calls the *praeminentia dignitatis*, and this produces the *praeminentia virtutis* or jurisdiction. St. Thomas likewise states that the spiritual power of the Church is based *in aliqua consecratione*, a consecration that exists in the first place for the eucharist, then for the other sacraments as liturgical actions, and finally for pastoral care.

The distinction between the powers of orders and of jurisdiction will certainly have to stay, but they should no longer be considered two totally distinct realities, because jurisdiction is subordinate to orders since it springs from it and serves it. This service, being juridical in kind, is carried out through the medium of authority, from which it follows that the acts of the power of orders are frequently conditioned by the exercise of jurisdiction, even in what concerns their very validity. But jurisdiction supposes a hierarchical consecration and is based on the sacramental character of holy orders. The canonical mission does not create power, but supposes it by virtue of its basic sacramentality, which is sometimes active (holy orders) and sometimes passive (baptism of the laity into a common priesthood). As Brousseau has said, the kingship of Christ is ordered to his priesthood. In the same way, the pastoral authority of the Church serves the sanctifying mission she exercises through her sacramental power.

The powers and laws of the Church are in fact ordered to this end—even those that at first sight seem furthest away from the sacraments, such as those governing tribunals and ecclesiastical goods. A good number of these rules have no immediate theological support, but are the product of natural justice and the judicial customs of each country; this is the case of civil laws that have passed into Canon Law. But even in these cases the law of the Church cannot dissociate itself from its sacramental meaning, since it exists to rule the People of God, a sanctifying society, worshiping God the Father through the Son in the Holy Spirit. This is why the revision of the Codex should bring out more clearly the connection and dependence between the ecclesiastical hierarchy and the sacrament of orders, since the present Codex makes orders and jurisdiction independent of each other, and the actual physical distance that separates some rules from others accentuates this impression of disconnectedness. Even the rights and duties of the clergy could be given next to the sacrament of orders, as deriving from it and being required by it, rather than, as at present, being merely disciplinary rules.

IV
THE SACRAMENTS AS A FUNCTION OF THE CHURCH

The foregoing has dealt with the sacraments as institution, corresponding to the constitutional aspect of the Church's law. When the sacrament is realized in an individual, it functions as an action of the Church, by which the saving act of Christ is made present in the person receiving the sacrament.

Seeing the sacrament in this way as a function of the Church is to take the viewpoint of the Codex and so to consider what is called sacramental law and liturgical law. Here the rules of Part I of Book III of the Codex apply, and also some of the penal clauses, such as cc. 2261 and 2364-74. I have already shown how what is basic in these rules should be transferred to the constitutional section. All that can be said about these rules here is that it is most important to insist on their basis in theology.

This functional aspect of the sacraments shows what is dynamic and contingent in the Church, just as the basic norms indicate what is fundamental and permanent. The sacramental sign is repeated and happens every time the sacrament is used; this sign is only sanctifying if its basic roots are in the Church, the permanent sacrament. Sacramentality only has meaning in a human context, because the sacraments exist to bring about a relationship between God and man. Man happens; he has a history—yet not so much a history as a structure, with a permanent consciousness of his personality. His existence comes about moment by moment in the flux of time. If sacramentality is to respond to human characteristics, it too has to be an organism with a permanent structure, but bringing about its happenings within the compass of the human event. God comes to meet our great human experiences in the sacraments, because "until there is a new heaven and a new earth where justice dwells, the pilgrim Church in her sacraments and institutions, which pertain to this present time, takes on the appearance of this passing world" (*Constitution on the Church*, n. 48).

Otto Ter Reegen, S.S.S./*Nijmegen, Netherlands*

The Rights of the Laity

We all know the notorious passage from the *Decretum Gratianum:* [1] "[Of the two classes in the Church] the first consists of those who by prayer and contemplation devote themselves to spiritual service; they withdraw from all earthly solicitude, and these are the priests and the monks. The second class consists of the laity; they are allowed to marry, to till the land, to institute tribunals, to bring their sacrifices to the altar, to pay the tithes. These people can be saved if they avoid all vices by doing what is right." According to this passage the layman is therefore a second-grade Christian. As J. Grotaers puts it pungently: "We, layfolk, are emerging from a state of excommunication." [2] He then lists five fields in which this excommunication was operative: theology, Scripture, spirituality, liturgy and communion under both kinds.

The documents of Vatican Council II, however, plainly show that this excommunication of the laity is now really a thing of the past. They rather suggest a change from a hierarchical Church to a Church of the laity. The concept of the "active participation of

[1] This is the first codification of Church law by the Camaldolese monk Gratian, in the middle of the 12th century, and it has never been declared official by the Church. The quotation is taken from Dr. Jan Grotaers, "De Leek in de teksten van Vaticanum II," in *Concilie in kort bestek* (Roermond, 1966), p. 182.

[2] *Ibid.,* p. 183.

16

the faithful" (*actuosa participatio fidelium*) in the *Constitution on the Sacred Liturgy* plays a part in practically all the conciliar documents and so becomes one of the features of the post-conciliar period where the starting point is no longer a one-sided emphasis on the hierarchy but the scriptural argument that, through baptism, all the baptized "are a chosen race, a royal priesthood, a holy nation, God's own people".[3] Hence all the faithful, including the clergy, are equal as members of the Church, whatever function they exercise, because all are equally subject to the authority of Christ and his Word. For this reason they must first of all respect and guarantee one another's freedom and co-responsibility. Whatever the relationships within the Church may be, this basic equality must always come first.[4] This recognition means a revolution in the appreciation of the layman's place and function in the Church. I want to try to indicate the rights of the laity in the spirit of the conciliar documents of Vatican Council II rather than define them strictly or formulate them.

1. *The Rights of the Laity in General*

The basic equality of all the faithful, based on baptism, implies also the communal responsibility of all for the Church and her pastoral mission in the world. The Church, therefore, can only fulfill her mission by the mutual cooperation and interaction of all the faithful. The universal and the special priesthood depend upon each other. Both participate, each in its own way, in the priesthood of Christ.[5] Both share equally in the prophetic function of the Lord, though the functions are different.

The layman is therefore essentially involved in all that touches the Church and in all that the Church does. He is increasingly aware of the fact that he is wholly involved in the Church's salvific mission in the world. This means that the old canonical rule must be put into operation again, which says that "what

[3] 1 Pet. 2, 9.
[4] *Stellingen en aanbevelingen over de werking van het gezag* (Pastoraal Concilie van de Nederlandse Kerkprovincie), n. 12.
[5] *Constitution on the Church*, n. 10.

concerns all must be treated and approved by all" (*quod omnibus tangit, abomnibus tractari et approbari debet*).[6] In modern language this means that the dialogue and discussion of ecclesiastical issues with the laity are not an open question but a basic right to which the layman is entitled. Put more sharply, it means that the Church cannot fulfill her mission without the active participation of the faithful. When the situation is seen in this light we realize that the contrast and too rigidly maintained distinction between function and no-function, between cleric and layman, disappears. Instead of opposing them, they should be seen as functionally related, each having his own function and his own place, but neither able to discharge his function without a constant dialogue with the other, without listening to the other.[7]

If, therefore, I speak explicitly of the rights of the laity, this is in no way an attempt to strip the official of his own rights; I only want to see how far there is room for the rights of the laity in this interplay implied in the Church's pastoral function, and to show that, in spite of difference in functions, rights and obligations, there must exist a mutual collegiality. The collegiality which exists between pope and bishops, between bishops and priests, and among priests themselves, must be extended to the laity.

2. *The Rights of the Laity in the Church's Mission*

(a) *Preaching.* When the Lord departed from this earth, he charged the Church with the preaching of the Gospel to all men.[8] This is a constitutive commission which affects all the faithful, without distinction of rank, status or function, and which binds them all.[9] The *Constitution on the Church* indicates that, in virtue of his participation in Christ's prophetic function, the layman, too, is called upon to preach: "Christ, the great prophet, who proclaimed the kingdom of his Father by the testimony of his life and the power of his words, continually fulfills his prophetic office until his full glory is revealed. He does this

---

[6] C. 5, L. LX, 5 and 7; LX, 1, 23.
[7] *Constitution on the Church*, n. 37.
[8] Mt. 28, 18-20.
[9] 1 Pet. 2, 9.

not only through the hierarchy who teach in his name and with his authority, but also through the laity. For that very purpose he made them his witnesses and gave them understanding of the faith and the grace of speech (cf. Acts 2, 17-18; Rev. 19, 10), so that the power of the Gospel might shine forth in their daily social and family life." [10] This can be called preaching, in the broad sense of the word, or secular evangelization. In order that this preaching in word and deed (the heart of the lay apostolate; cf. the *Decree on the Apostolate of the Laity*) can be genuine, inspired, credible and comprehensible to man, the faithful must be guided and supported in this by the official functionary, who must introduce them deeper into the mysteries of the faith and help them to practice their faith in a contemporary way.[11] He could not discharge this function without a sound formation and catechization of adults. Here lies a new function for the official functionary.

The question nevertheless arises whether laymen cannot explicitly participate in the Church's preaching in the strict sense of the word. The Code of Canon Law allows them to catechize [12] but forbids them to preach at the celebration of the eucharist,[13] although Paul said that the ordinary faithful can also speak at the religious service, each according to the charisma with which he is endowed.[14] When the *Dogmatic Constitution on the Church* says that "some of them [the laity] do all they can to provide sacred services when sacred ministers are lacking or are blocked by a persecuting regime",[15] it does not seem unreasonable to conclude that the layman can assume the function of preaching in the strict sense. This is not based on a question of delegation but on his actual belonging to the Church; in other words, it is a basic right which the Church cannot deny him, but which the official authority can more closely define for the building up of

[10] *Constitution on the Church*, n. 35; cf. *Decree on the Apostolate of the Laity*, n. 6.
[11] *Decree on the Apostolate of the Laity*, n. 25.
[12] *Codex Iuris Canonici* (*C.I.C.*), c. 1333.
[13] *C.I.C.*, c. 1342, par. 2.
[14] 1 Cor. 14, 26.
[15] *Constitution on the Church*, n. 35.

the body, the Church. That is why the proper authority should consider whether and how the lay person, man or woman, can be used for official preaching in an age when interest in the Church is decreasing, when there is an increasing lack of priests and a growing number of lay theologians. Charismatic gifts could find recognition in the restoration of lay preachers. This would imply that the layman should have more opportunities to enroll in faculties of theology. The office is indeed especially commissioned to preach, but this commission is not exclusive in any sense.

As, on the one hand, the Church's faith must be put into the preaching, and, on the other, the contents can only be understood in a collective listening to it, the whole community must be involved in the discussion of the content, meaning and formulation of the data of faith. In both content and preaching, the expression of the faith cannot take place without the active contribution of the ordinary faithful. "The body of the faithful as a whole, anointed as they are by the Holy One (cf. Jn. 2, 20. 27), cannot err in matters of belief. Thanks to a supernatural sense of the faith which characterizes the People as a whole, it manifests this unerring quality when, 'from the bishops down to the last member of the laity', it shows universal agreement in matters of faith and morals." [16] This implies that the laity cannot be excluded there where the Church reflects in faith upon her nature, her message, her function and her place in the world. Strictly speaking, this means that the layman should therefore be invited to ecumenical and provincial councils as well as diocesan synods and be admitted there, not merely as an observer, but as a voting member. As proof we have the oldest councils, beginning with that of Jerusalem. How this presence of the laity should be arranged is of course a debatable question. One could maintain that they are represented in the person of the diocesan bishop as the first of the local faithful (one may well doubt whether this is in fact true), but one would have to admit that this is hardly wholly satisfactory insofar as the rights of the laity are con-

[16] *Ibid.*, n. 12.

cerned. Why should every diocesan bishop on his way to the ecumenical council not be accompanied by a lay person chosen from the diocesan pastoral councils, and, once admitted, be entitled to full voting rights as a full member? The Dutch have accepted the layman as a full member in their pastoral councils.

In the light of what has been said, one rightly concludes that binding ecclesiastical statements on faith and practice must be reached in dialogue and discussion with the community of believers. In representing the believing community, the laity do not have to accept a unilateral statement by the hierarchy as an ecclesiastical statement. In order to be able to hear the voice of the laity and to sound their "sense of faith" (*sensus fidei*), discussion groups, such as they are organized in Holland, are of the utmost importance. There the faithful aim at giving conscious expression to their membership in the Church, at deepening their faith in conversation with each other and at articulating this faith in contemporary language. This is why official authorities cannot take up a neutral position with regard to these groups. Even when a binding ecclesiastical statement results from this dialogue and discussion with the believing community, every believer retains the right to decide whether he will accept it or not in personal freedom and according to the honest judgment of his conscience.[17] The Church will have to reckon with the various modalities of belief that exist among men, so that excommunication on the ground of "not believing" must be considered a thing of the past.

By the same token one cannot deny the layman's right to criticize and correct the proclamation. He should have the possibility to question an authority who preaches opinions which run counter to the sense of faith of the community, *via* the parochial council, for instance, or that of the deanery or that of the diocese. If necessary he should be able to warn such an authority and, in consultation with the bishop, have him deposed or transferred. If the bishop would not cooperate, there would be the possibility of appealing to Rome. Although the preacher has his

[17] *Stellingen en aanbevelingen* (as above), n. 28.

own responsibility in addressing the community instructively, evangelical sensibility and care demand that he do so prudently, carefully and gently, so that the faithful will not get confused and uncertain.

This reckoning with the sense of faith of the community consists not only in discussing matters of faith, but also matters of the community's daily conduct, the approval or disapproval of certain practices, attitudes and opinions that may have prevailed up to that time. When, for instance, a fair number of serious believers live their marriage in ways that differ from those so far propounded by the Church, this may be a sign of authentic Christian awareness, and cannot be glibly ignored.

(b) *The Celebration of the Liturgy.* Nowhere has the "active participation of the faithful" been so clearly formulated and worked out as in the *Constitution on the Sacred Liturgy.*[18] All the faithful play their own part in the liturgical action; the functions do not cut across each other. Everyone takes part in his own special way.[19] The liturgy must be celebrated in such a way that the believer is actively involved, not as spectator but as an "actor". The liturgy, indeed, is the cultic action of the Church in which the whole Church is involved in all her structures—hence the urgency with which the Constitution exhorts bishops and priests to devote themselves to the renewal of the liturgy.[20]

If the layman takes part as an actor in the celebration, the question arises whether and how he can be drawn into the preparation of it, so that the shape of the celebration may also be molded by his positive contribution and his wishes as well as his grievances. He must have some say in the work of the team that composes and shapes every week at least the liturgy of the Sunday, and this not primarily because of his expertise but principally because of his being a believer. It would be worthwhile to ask the opinion not only of the "good" Catholic, but also of the Catholic who is outside or on the fringe of the Church. Only the layman can ensure that the liturgy becomes "secular" in the

[18] *Constitution on the Sacred Liturgy,* nn. 14, 30, 48, 50.
[19] *Ibid.,* n. 28.
[20] *Ibid.,* nn. 14-20.

sense of corresponding to everyday life. The liturgy is too heavily
controlled by the specialists, but it can only be shaped by a celebration which is inspired by genuine faith. This postulates a
much wider scope for experimenting so that the believer will
again live the liturgy as part of his real life. Does he not have the
right to insist that more attention should be paid to his experience of the faith than to all kinds of historical facets that have,
for a large part, lost any meaning for the present? This integration of the laity cannot rest satisfied with the mere possibility of
lay members of institutes for pastoral liturgy which assist the
national liturgical commission in its work.[21]

Although the *Constitution on the Sacred Liturgy* insists that
some sacramentals can, at least in special circumstances and in
the judgment of the ordinary, be administered by lay people who
have the suitable ability for this,[22] it gives no answer to the
question whether and how far the layman can administer the
sacraments and preside over the liturgical assembly. On this
point there is no difficulty in two sacraments, that of baptism and
that of marriage. In the absence of a priest or deacon, anyone
can baptize in case of emergency.[23] At least in the Western
Church, the partners themselves administer the sacrament of
marriage to each other. But what about the other sacraments?
Insofar as the sacrament of penance is concerned, it is certain
that, in the beginning, not only the official authority administered this sacrament. Those inspired by the Spirit (*pneumatici*),
martyrs and confessors claimed the right to forgive sins in that
period.[24] Moreover, lay confession existed until far in the Middle Ages, and great theologians admitted its sacramental value.[25]
In Corinth the faithful shared with Paul the right to administer
discipline (cf. 1 Cor. 5, 4-5).

In the Pauline Church, it appears that the ordinary believer
was not precluded from administering the eucharist, so that there

21 *Ibid.*, n. 44.
22 *Ibid.*, n. 79.
23 *Ibid.*, n. 68.
24 H. Küng, *The Church* (London and New York, 1967).
25 *Ibid.*

is here no question of administration being tied up with an official function. In times of need, when there is no priest or he is absent for a considerable time, the possibility exists therefore of a community celebrating the eucharist under the presidency of a lay person. In a time when the "popular" Church makes way for the Church of the "committed", this possibility may well have to be put into practice. Why should a father of a family not administer this sacrament in special circumstances? It also seems possible that the community itself, again in special circumstances, should appoint somebody from among themselves to lead in Word and sacrament, and thus call on a lay person to act as official functionary. In times of persecution and crucial scarcity of priests, the Church may well have to give clear directives on how far the laity may put this basic right into practice.

In the same way, the community may refuse to let somebody take part in the sacraments (cf. 1 Cor. 5, 4-5). But this also means that the community can admit people who are excluded today by Canon Law, such as persons living in concubinage.

3. *The Rights of the Laity in Church Government*

(a) *The Right To Appoint.* Like every other organization, the Church cannot do without administrators who are at the service of the community. Sometimes they represent the community, and sometimes they stand over against the community. On the one hand, the ecclesiastical officials receive their power from the community, on the other, from the Lord himself. Since all good government demands that the community be involved in one way or another, it is necessary to integrate the laity in ecclesiastical government. This can be done in various ways. It should be normal that the choice of his leaders should not be made behind his back. This applies to every level of government: pope, bishop, dean and parish priest, according to the principle laid down by Leo I: "He who wants to be at the head of all must be chosen by all." [26] The parish priest might be chosen by or in consultation with the parish council, and the dean by the deanery

---

[26] *Ibid.*

council, and the bishop should not be appointed without at least consulting the diocesan pastoral council. Why should the pope not be chosen by an international pastoral council in which bishops, priests, lay people and religious take part? We should therefore create, at every level, consultative bodies that can operate in the choice of an official.[27] Once the layman has a say in the appointment, he must also have a say in the matters of deposition, replacement or dismissal. Justified grievances about an official must be dealt with. If necessary, a council of appeal should be set up.

(b) *Councils of Administration.* In order to involve the laity in Church government, Vatican Council II expressed the wish that in all dioceses the bishop should set up a pastoral council, consisting of priests, lay people and religious, in order to advise the bishop in his pastoral function.[28] This has been done in many dioceses.[29] Members are chosen either by election (all, or a number of them) or by episcopal appointment (also either all, or a number of them).[30] In certain cases the bishop can give the lay members the active vote,[31] although, according to the Motu Proprio *Ecclesiae sanctae* they only play an advisory part.[32] The democratization of the Church implies, however, that members should have an active vote in all business. These advisory bodies should be set up at every level so that the layman should be in a position to contribute to the self-fulfillment of the Church. This is the only way in which the dialogue can be institutionalized.[33]

I said "at every level". Just as every diocese has a pastoral council, so each episcopal conference (whether regional, na-

[27] *Stellingen en aanbevelingen* (as above), n. 38.
[28] *Decree on the Pastoral Office of the Bishops in the Church*, n. 27; cf. Motu Proprio *Ecclesiae Sanctae*, nn. 15-16.
[29] *Senatus Presbyterorum et Consilium Pastorale* (Edited by the Pastoral Inst. of the Dutch Province). Cf. F. Klostermann, "Nieuwe strukturen in het bisdom," in *Theologie en Pastoraat* 63, n. 6 (1967), pp. 348-60, esp. p. 355; this has also appeared in *Diakonia* 2 (1967), pp. 257-70.
[30] Cf. n. 28.
[31] Motu Proprio *Ecclesiae Sanctae*, n. 16.
[32] Cf. n. 30.
[33] *Stellingen en aanbevelingen* (see above), n. 25.

tional or international), and even the episcopal synod, should have its own pastoral council. Just as the conferences appoint bishops for the episcopal synod, so the members of the pastoral council or the episcopal synod could be appointed by the subordinate councils. In this way we could integrate the whole Church in the matter of government. This would be more satisfactory than the institution of a separate council, such as the lay council.[34] If the pastoral councils function properly, the function of the lay council is superfluous. Just as the diocesan pastoral council must be rounded off at the top by a superstructure, so it must have an infrastructure at the bottom, in the deanery and parish councils. The *Decree on the Apostolate of the Laity* [35] offers the laity a possible membership in the Roman dicasteries—at least, so it appears, as consultants.[36] Nothing is said about the layman being appointed prefect or secretary, although such an appointment would be important, particularly to such posts as require secular expertise, such as finance and statistics.

(c) *Ecclesiastical Functions.* According to Canon 118 only the clergy can have jurisdiction and thus be eligible to perform ecclesiastical functions. This regulation, however, is a mere matter of Canon Law, a symptom of the clericalization of the Church. It should therefore be abolished so that qualified laymen can have access to ecclesiastical functions such as those of vicar-general, *officialis*, synodal or prosynodal judge. Is it necessary that the leaders in the faith should have *per se* the highest degree of jurisdictional power? Can the layman be the highest administrator in diocese and Church? Ecclesiastical sources are not very clear on the point whether the highest function in the Church implies necessarily the highest degree of authority. Connected with this issue is the question whether the layman can be the leader of the local community. The Pauline Church of Corinth and the Churches of the Reformation give here an affirmative answer. The fact that in the early centuries several emperors

---

[34] Motu Proprio *Catholicam Christi Ecclesiam*, June 1, 1967.
[35] Canon 222.
[36] Apost. Const. *Regimini Universae Ecclesiae*, n. 5.

summoned and presided over Church councils points in the same direction. The exclusive right of the pope to summon ecumenical councils should therefore be allowed to lapse or be formulated differently in the revised Code of Canon Law.

(d) *Administration of Church Property.* According to Canons 1520 and 1521, §2, the layman can share in the administration of Church property. One might wonder, however, whether the whole administration should not be put into the hands of the laity, the more so since they are on the whole better equipped in these matters than Church officials.

Since Church property as such also belongs to the community, it should be stipulated that the faithful receive every year a balance sheet and explanation of the state of this Church property. Moreover, every year or every two years at fixed times the community, particularly the advisory bodies, should be presented with a budget.

It is desirable that at every level of pastoral care a financial commission should be set up, consisting of qualified lay people, who either will advise the bishop in the conduct of the administration or, in the name of the Church—parish, deanery, diocese and the universal Church—will administer the finances autonomously.

Conclusion

Looking at the problem as a whole, one reaches the conclusion that in the Church of Christ there is no difference in the rights of those who hold office and those who do not, lay people and clergy. If there are nevertheless different and distinct rights, then these rights are only based on the function.

What we have come to call *de jure divino* (of divine right) in the course of the centuries might well appear on closer study to be no more than ecclesiastical right, based not on some essential difference between office and lack of office, on clergy and laity, but only on the functional distinction required for the healthy growth of the body of Christ, the Church.

Antonio Mostaza Rodríguez/*Valencia, Spain*

The Minister of Confirmation

I
UP TO THE EIGHTH CENTURY

During the early centuries of Christianity, it was the bishop who used to administer the rites of Christian initiation—baptism, confirmation and the eucharist.[1] In theological terminology, we would say that the bishop was at that time the ordinary minister (or the "original" minister, as Vatican Council II describes it) of confirmation as well as of the remaining sacraments.[2] No presbyter in the bishop's city was permitted to fulfill any priestly function without his prior dispensation.

The increase in numbers of the Christian faithful which resulted from the peace under Constantine made it necessary for presbyters and, occasionally, even deacons, to be entrusted with the evangelization of centers of rural population and, in addition, small cities where it was not granted to establish bishoprics, "so that the prestige and authority of bishops might not suffer decline".[3] Given the impossibility of the task for the bishop, such presbyters and deacons, by necessity, were obliged to baptize the catechumens in these rural and urban communities; and since confirmation was conferred immediately after baptism,

---

[1] The reader will find the sources for this in my monograph, *The Problem of the Extraordinary Minister of Confirmation* (Salamanca, 1952), 386; cf. also J. Neumann, *Spender der Firmung* (Meitingen, 1963); F. X. Dölger, *Das Sakrament der Firmung* (Wien, 1906).

[2] *Constitution on the Church*, n. 26.

[3] Synod of Sardica (A.D. 343), c. 6; Mansi, *Saer. Concil. nova et ampl. Collectio*, 3, 10.

28

there was no solution but to give presbyters the faculty of confirming or, alternatively, to separate the two rites, reserving the ministry of confirmation for the bishop. The Roman Church settled for the second alternative, while the Eastern Churches and those of Spain and Gaul adopted the first.

1. In the Roman Church, then, those baptized by presbyters had to present themselves to the bishop in order to receive confirmation from his hands. And yet, in addition to the fact that not all the Western Churches adopted this practice, not even the Churches in the Roman province adhered to it from the very beginning, since in some of them it was the presbyters who still administered confirmation. This occured in Gubbio (Umbria), its bishop being informed in a letter from Innocent I (416) that "only for bishops is it licit to mark with the sign of the cross".[4] In spite of this decree—the first pontifical document which declares the administering of confirmation by presbyters to be "illicit"—presbyters in Lucania and Sicily were continuing the practice at the end of the same century, which led Gelasius I to prevent them from assuming this faculty. Nevertheless, even this new edict fell short of total success; a century later we find presbyters in Cagliari (Sardinia) still exercising this function, as shown by the decree issued in 593 by Gregory the Great to Januarius, the bishop of the diocese, prohibiting them the ministry.[5] This measure provoked serious discontent among Sardinian presbyters. long accustomed as they were to administering the sacrament, and the Benedictine pope, hearing of it, wrote again to their bishop in 594, authorizing them to continue exercising the faculty in the absence of a bishop, but, at the same time, justifying his earlier prohibition on the grounds that it conformed with the custom of his Church.[6]

2. In the Spanish Church, numerous documents, from the 4th century onward, testify to the custom of presbyters confirming when baptizing in the absence of a bishop or, during his presence, by his dispensation. Even deacons appear to have been

---

[4] Innocent I, *Epist. ad Decentium*, III, 6: *PL* 20, 554-55.
[5] Gregory the Great, *Epist. ad Januarium: PL* 77, 667.
[6] *Ibid.: PL* 77, 696; cf. A, Mostaza, *op. cit.*, 18-20.

authorized to exercise this faculty when baptizing in danger of death, in the absence of a bishop or presbyter.[7] This custom survived in Spain until the abolition of the Mozarabic liturgy at the end of the 11th century.[8]

3. As regards the Church in Gaul, ample evidence shows that, from the 5th century onward, presbyters, and deacons as well, could confirm. According to Pseudo-Jerome, "the power to confirm and to administer all the divine sacraments duly pertains to presbyters, and for reasons of discipline alone are the ordination of clerics and the consecration of virgins, churches and chrism reserved for the bishops".[9] The Council of Riez, in 439, mentions among the rights of the presbyter "that of confirming neophytes in the church for which he is ordained".[10] In early Christian history, there are many documents which attribute the origin of the bishops' prerogative of confirmation in the Latin Church to ecclesiastical ruling, while none is found which would make it derive from divine institution.[11]

4. With regard to the Eastern Churches, complete evidence supports the fact that, from the 4th century onward, both bishops and presbyters, indiscriminately, could administer confirmation. For St. John Chrysostom and St. Epiphanius, "bishops are superior to presbyters only by their power of ordaining", and Macarius of Jerusalem affirms that the power of confirming is exclusive to bishops and presbyters. Eastern liturgical books support this testimony.[12] Finally, St. Jerome, well acquainted with the customs of both East and West, also stipulates that presbyters share in all the episcopal functions, except that of ordaining.[13]

[7] Synod of Elvira, cc. 38 and 77; Mansi, *op. cit.*, 2, 12 and 18; First Council of Toledo, c. 20; Mansi, *op. cit.*, 3, 1002; A. Mostaza, *op. cit.*, 24-39.
[8] Cf. *Liber Ordinum*, ed. M. Ferotin (Paris, 1904), 34.
[9] *Ibid.*, *De septum ordinibus Ecclesiae*, VI: *PL* 30, 155.
[10] *Ibid.*, c, 4, ed. C. Munier, *Corp. Christ.*, 148, 68.
[11] Cf. Mostaza, *op. cit.*, 9f.
[12] St. John Chrysostom, *Homil. II in Timoth.*: *PG* 62, 553; St. Epiphanius, *Adv. Haer.*, III, 15: *PG* 42, 508; *Can.* Macarii Hierosol., c. 4; Mai, *Script. vet. nova Collectio*, Vol. 10, 271; H. Denzinger, *Ritus Orientalium*, I (Würzburg, 1863), 61f.; Assemani, *Codex lit. Eccles. universae*, III (Paris and Leipzig, 1902), 56f.
[13] *Ibid.*, *Epist. 146 ad Evangelum*: *PL* 22, 119.

II

FROM THE EIGHTH CENTURY TO THE COUNCIL OF TRENT:
APPEARANCE OF THE EXTRAORDINARY MINISTER

1. Between the 8th and 12th centuries, Roman disciplines were being imposed on all the Western Churches except in Spain, where the old customs survived. Documents of this period attribute the privilege of confirming to bishops alone. Conciliar decrees, as well as many false edicts, give support in general to this episcopal prerogative, in opposition to the *chorepiscopi* whose confirmations were considered invalid by Isaac de Langres and by the decree of Pseudo-Eusebius.[14] This famous text, forged by Pseudo-Isidore, strongly affirms that only bishops can confer valid confirmation.

Writers of this period, as well as the Synod of Worms in 868, attribute the episcopal privilege of confirming to ecclesiastical legislation, the author of which would have been Pope Sylvester.[15] To this pope also is attributed the origin of anointing conferred by presbyters, which, in the view of Carolingian commentators, differs from that imposed by bishops only in that the latter enriches the soul more than the former.[16] In both anointings they discern the operation of the Holy Spirit, while Pseudo-Bede goes so far as to recognize equal efficacy in both, and to declare, with some anger, that the second—among other privileges—has been reserved for bishops *propter arrogantiam*.[17]

2. Between the 12th century and the Council of Trent, the practice of confirmation exclusively by bishops became so estab-

---

[14] Isaac de Langres, *Canones*, tit. II, c. 30: *PL* 124, 1109; Pseudo-Eusebius, *Epist. ad episc. Campaniae*, ed. Hinschius, 242.

[15] Cf. Synod of Worms, c. 8; Mansi, *op. cit.*, 15, 871; Amalarius of Metz, *De eccles. off.*, 27: *PL* 105, 1041-49; Ratramnus, *Contra Graecorum opposita*, 1. 4, c. 7: *PL* 121, 333-34; Rabanus Maurus, *De clericorum inst.*, I, 28: *PL* 107, 312; *Liber Pontificalis*, ed. Duchesne, I (Paris, 1886), 76-77.

[16] *Ibid.*; cf. Mostaza, *op. cit.*, 62f.

[17] Pseudo-Bede, *In Psalm.*, 26: *PL* 93, 614.

lished in the West that the older administration under which presbyters could confirm almost passed from memory.[18] Because of this oblivion, and because of the extension of Gregory the Great's earlier concession by a decree of Gratian, together with other pontifical documents which deny this office to presbyters—in particular the decree of Pseudo-Eusebius and its unhappy influence in this question—the problem arose in the second half of the 12th century as to whether it *was* the exclusive right of bishops to confirm, and whether it *was* possible for presbyters to administer the sacrament with pontifical dispensation. How was one to reconcile the blatant contradiction between the attitudes of Pope Gregory and Pseudo-Eusebius, his supposed predecessor? Could bishops alone confirm, or was it possible for the pope to confer this ministry on one who was not a bishop? This was the question confronting theologians and canon lawyers. The latter, with some exceptions, concurred in recognizing the pope's authority to confer this ministry on presbyters, but they failed to agree in determining precisely who could qualify for such a ministry—whether a priest alone, or other clerics also, or even confirmed lay people; nor could they resolve whether confirmation was reserved for bishops by divine institution or by ecclesiastical mandate, although the majority inclined to the latter view.[19]

For theologians, the problem was even more complex, with the result that they could not even reach agreement in recognizing the pope's power to confer this ministry on presbyters. Many (Albert the Great, Biel, Durandus, Mair, etc.) deny this authority, in opposition to the large majority.[20] Those who support the thesis base their argument—through ignorance of the old custom in the Greek Church and in some Western Churches

[18] The only exception is in the diocese of Würzburg, where presbyters appear to be still confirming, in cases of danger of death, up to the second half of the 15th century, in spite of repeated prohibitions. Cf. F. X. Dölger, *op cit.*

[19] Cf. A. Mostaza, *op. cit.*, 75-99; F. Gillmann, *Zur Lehere der Scholastik von Spender der Firmung, und des Weihesakraments* (Paderborn, 1920).

[20] Cf. A. Mostaza, *op. cit.*, 103-177.

of confirmation by presbyters—almost entirely on St. Gregory's concession, some, with Richard Fitzralph, believing that presbyters require this papal dispensation only for the sake of licitness. This opinion attracted supporters up to the end of the last century, and was considered probable by Dölger at the beginning of the present century.[21]

III
FROM THE COUNCIL OF TRENT TO THE PRESENT DAY

1. The Council of Trent does not touch upon the question of the extraordinary minister. It limits itself to defining that "the bishop alone is the ordinary minister of confirmation, and not any priest", without discussing the concept of "ordinary" minister—meaning here a minister *ex officio* and not one who possesses the power to confirm validly and without pontifical dispensation, by virtue of his ordination, as against the "extraordinary" minister, who, according to the unfounded claims forwarded by many writers, would lack this power.[22]

2. Even after the Council of Trent, the viewpoint which would deny the extraordinary ministry of presbyters has distinguished support (Alfonso de Castro, de Soto, Estius, etc.), but the large majority of authors uphold the affirmative thesis, which became popular during the 18th and 19th centuries. According to Martín de Ledesma and A. Salmerón, not only the pope, but also bishops—by virtue of divine law—can entrust this ministry to presbyters, an opinion to which many authors have allied themselves to the present day.[23]

3. As the medieval popes had done, the Holy See continued

---

[21] On the appalling ignorance of the medieval Latin authors regarding the Greek presbyters' custom of confirming, cf. the response of the Armenian bishops to the "Catalogue of Errors" surrounding confirmation, which theologians drew up at the request of Benedict XII, toward the middle of the 14th century, in Mansi, *op. cit.*, 25, 1185 and 1240-41; Dölger, 218, n. 1.

[22] Cf. A. Mostaza, *op. cit.*, 183-235.

[23] *Ibid.*, 241f.

to oppose the practice of confirmation by presbyters in the Eastern Church, but as long as separated Churches returned to the fold, they were permitted to retain the custom, as had been granted by the Church Fathers at the Council of Florence.[24] Except for the Italo-Greeks and the Maronites, all other Catholics observing Eastern rites obtained recognition of this custom from Rome during the 18th and 19th centuries.[25]

4. In the Latin Church, after the Council of Trent, and particularly from the 18th century onward, pontifical authorization for presbyters to fulfill this ministry became more frequent, as in the case of missionaries and some priests in Latin America and the Philippines; but such concessions were made under an extremely restrictive scrutiny, and many were the faithful who died without receiving the sacrament of confirmation.[26]

5. The Code of Canon Law provides no remedy for this necessity by appointing certain extraordinary ministers under law itself (c. 782, §3), and unfortunately Fr. Wernz did not succeed in guiding his projected canon, which would have authorized parish priests to confirm in danger of death, to a successful conclusion.[27]

6. A significant change in the traditional ruling of the Latin Church on the ministry of confirmation was introduced by Pius XII through his decree *Spiritus Sancti munera* of 1946. By this decree, authority to confirm in danger of death resulting from illness is given to priests with their own parishes, actual vicars, administrators, and priests who have exclusive and regular charge of souls, with all the rights and duties of parish priests.[28]

[24] Council of Florence, Mansi, *ed. cit.*, 31, 1039-40.

[25] Cf. R. Souarn, "De presbytero or. confir. ministro," in *Jus Pontificium* II (1931), 131-43; A. Mostaza, *op. cit.*, 317f.

[26] On the severity of the Roman curia's criteria for granting such concessions, cf., for example, *Thesaurus resol. quae in causis prop. apud S.C. Interp. prodierunt*, Vol. 16 (Rome, 1868), nn. 23, 27-30, pp. 30-32; S. C. de Sacr., *In una Namurcensi et al.* (1924): *AAS* 27 (1924), 14; U. Navarrete, "De ministris extr. confirm. in Amer. Lat. et Ins. Phillip.," in *Periodica*, 49 (1960), 143.

[27] Cf. Zerba, *Comment. in D. Spiritus S. munera* (Rome, 1947), 33-34.

[28] S. C. de Prop. Fide, *Decr. Spir. S. munera: AAS* 38 (1946), 349-54; T. J. Quinn, *The Extraordinary Minister of Confirmation According to the Most Recent Decrees of the S. Congr.* (Rome, 1951).

Complementing this decree is the *Post Latum* decree of 1947, in which the Congregation *de Propaganda Fide* gives power to ordinaries in the missions to authorize this ministry for all priests having charge of souls; similarly, the decree of the Congregation for the Eastern Church (1948) permits Latin priests the use of this faculty, to be exercised with regard to those under their pastoral care who observe Eastern rites.[29] The valid exercise of the faculty granted by these decrees is subject to the condition that the minister act within the boundaries of his own territory and that he confer the sacrament on those in danger of death resulting from illness.

The outcome of these mandates and of the several subsequent rescripts which extend the ministry of confirmation to even more priests (military and hospital chaplains, etc.) is that the reception of the sacrament is greatly facilitated; nevertheless, the Latin faithful still enjoy conditions inferior to those under Eastern rites, including the separated Churches.

IV

SUGGESTIONS IN VIEW OF THE NEW RULING
AND REFLECTIONS ON THE PROBLEM OF THE EXTRAORDINARY MINISTER

1. For ecumenical reasons, and mindful of *salus animarum* above all, we would recommend that under the new Code, the prohibition to confirm which is imposed on presbyters should affect only the licitness and not the validity of the sacrament, and that all priests should be allowed to perform this ministry, without any impediment, for those in danger of death from whatever causes; in addition, we recommend that ordinaries should be authorized to entrust this function to certain presbyters of their diocese, who would assist them in administering the sacrament—this being the only way in which the Latin faithful could receive the sacrament before their first communion, as its nature demands and as a venerable tradition justifies.

[29] S. C. de Prop. Fide, Decr. *Post Latum: AAS* 40 (1948), 41; S. C. pro Eccles. Or., Decr. *Cum ex c. 782, 4: AAS* 40 (1948), 422.

2. We should like to comment, very briefly, on the serious problem which is presented by the extraordinary minister of confirmation, taking the hypothesis that he cannot validly exercise this ministry if not authorized to do so by law or by special pontifical appointment, the state of things as inferred from several documents of the ordinary magisterium, although none of these has the character of an *ex cathedra* definition.[30]

What does the priest lack, or what does he receive by this "appointment", in order to be able to confirm? In solving this problem, we believe that it is necessary to start from this premise —one of the conclusions to be drawn from this article, and especially from the massive documentation presented in our monograph—namely, that "the episcopal privilege of confirming is of ecclesiastical origin".[31] Bearing in mind the power of the Church over the sacraments "except in their substance", we need not take into account a large number of those who would query this problem. It is unnecessary to enter into profound expositions of either the nature of the presbyter's power to confirm or the nature of the power conferred by the pope. The pope, in authorizing this ministry for presbyters, is not, properly speaking, conferring any power; he is simply leaving free and open to them, by removing the ecclesiastical prohibition which was there, something which they possess by virtue of their ordination.

Inasmuch, then, as the conferring of this pontifical authorization is a juridical act, the Church makes provision, under Canon 209, for cases of positive or probable doubt as to whether such authorization should be given.[32]

[30] Cf., for example, Epist. *Ex quo* of Pius X. *AAS* (1911), 119; c. 782, 3 and 4, and the decrees already mentioned, *Spir. S. munera* and *Post Latum.*

[31] This conclusion is "evident" and "incontrovertible" for many distinguished canon lawyers and theologians who have studied our work. Cf., for example, D. van den Eynde, in *Antonianum* 31 (1955), 192-93; T. G. Barberena, in *Rev. Esp. de Der. Can.* 8 (1953), 655-58; O. Robleda, in *Estud. Ecles.* (1954), 248-49; J. A. Aldama, in *Salmanticensis* I (1954), 491f.

[32] Cf. A. Mostaza, "La potestad de confirmar en los ministros extraordinarios," in *Rev. Esp. de Der. Can.* 14 (1959), 503-516.

Eliseo Ruffini/*Como, Italy*

What Is the Proper Age To Receive Confirmation?

From the middle of the last century onward the problem of the age for the conferral of confirmation has come to the fore more than once, and it is logical that in the climate of post-conciliar renewal the question should be posed once again.[1] The conditions under which the Christian community is inserted into the contemporary world have immediately notable modifications, its function is nowadays more demanding, and the necessity for an authentically Christian witness is felt much more than in the past.

On the other hand, in order that the Church may be able to carry out all the tasks to which she is called, her members must attain a greater appreciation of the obligations deriving from their membership in the People of God. Since baptism has for many centuries been conferred at an age when it is not possible to assume one's responsibilities in reflective form, it seems logical that at least confirmation—in which Christian initiation is completed—should be imparted at a sufficiently advanced age.

Viewed in these terms, the problem appears to be easily soluble. In reality, however, it is much more complex. This is confirmed by the variations encountered in the legislation of the

[1] A rich bibliography in this respect will be found in the works cited in our article.

37

Latin Church, from the Council of Trent onward.[2] Every time
that circumstances analogous to our own have arisen, the decision to delay the age of confirmation has here and there been
taken, but then a reconsideration on the doctrinal level or even
the concrete experience of the inefficacy of such a provision has
almost always brought about a return to the more traditional
practice of conferring the sacrament at the age of discretion.

Papal documents and those of the Roman dicasteries can provide a few constants (legitimacy of confirmation conferred on
children before the use of reason; invitation to respect the
rhythm of baptism, confirmation and the eucharist) which seem
to suggest a certain solution, but this is not enough to provide
principles of a dogmatic order for the purposes of a sure decision. As a matter of fact, the practice has for some time developed outside these suggestions.

Furthermore, the fact that today psychology, pedagogy, cate-
chetics and religious sociology—in addition to pastoral theology
and dogma—evince interest in this question, as well as that each
of these sciences claims a certain priority of competence, enables
us to understand not only the complexity of the problem, but
also the diversity of the solutions and the inadequacy of some of
the perspectives. However, in our view, what renders the problem practically insoluble is the fact that it has been reduced principally to a question of age.

On this plane no solution will ever go beyond the confines of
opinion and the provisional. Everyone could have his reasons for
saying that the most suitable age for confirmation is the age of
discretion (6-8), childhood (8-10), adolescence (12-16), early
youth (17-20) and, finally, mature youth (20-30).[3] In such circumstances each of the sciences mentioned above will have the

[2] A. Adam, *Firmung und Seelsorge* (Düsseldorf, 1958); R. Levet,
"L'âge de la Confirmation dans la législation des diocèses de France
depuis le Concile de Trente," in *Maison-Dieu* 54 (1958), pp. 118-42; D.
Tettamanzi, "L'età della cresima nella disciplina della Chiesa latina," in
Scuola Catt. 95 (1967), pp. 34-61.

[3] Every one of these theses has been supported by a recent inquiry; cf.
"Um den rechten Zeitpunkt der Firmspendung," in *Diakonia* 1 (1966)
pp. 285-91.

full right to intervene in the debate and to suggest to ecclesiastical legislation the provisional but more opportune solution in accord with the times.

The only science with nothing to say will be dogmatic theology, for, already engaged in finding in revelation whatever is necessary for an adequate reflection on the sacrament of confirmation, it would not know where to find the dogmatic data to resolve a problem of age. Yet if there is anything which can justify the question and withdraw it from the category of problems that can have all kinds of solutions, it is whatever restores the problem to a dogmatic context. The real question is that of establishing the function of confirmation in Christian initiation: to see its relations with baptism and its finalization in the eucharist for the building up of the Church. Only afterward, on the basis of the principles established, can there be any consideration of the question of age.

Confirmation and Christian Initiation

There is such a convergence of doctrinal and historical data concerning the baptism-confirmation relation that it increases the temptation to magnify this relation rather than to minimize it. The circumstances that have led the Latin Church to separate the administration of confirmation from baptism are well known; we should, instead, recall that the separation has come about for practical, not doctrinal reasons.

At the basis of this practice—which was introduced slowly and only after several centuries of Christian life—undoubtedly lay the conviction that Christian initiation took place by means of two distinct sacraments, but the reflection on what distinguished them objectively over and above the single ritual distinction developed very late and not always in adequate form. Hence, when the Anglican theologian Gregory Dix advanced the hypothesis—no more than twenty years ago—that the baptism-confirmation relation is as close as the remission of sins (baptism) is to the gift of the Holy Spirit (confirmation), Catholics and Protestants became aware of how much still remained to be studied before the distinction of the two sacraments could be described in objective terms.[4]

Reflection on the discussion that followed and the orientations that guided it can lead to a specific teaching. In the wake of what had been done by the post-Tridentine theology of the sacraments, it was sought to determine even in this circumstance the distinction of confirmation from baptism on the basis of their effects. But through an error in perspective, account was taken predominantly of the effects of subjective sanctification, almost completely forgetting that every sacrament, and especially those of initiation, must also have effects of an ecclesial dimension. Various inconveniences resulted from this fact.

Even refuting the thesis of G. Dix which made baptism and confirmation two aspects of one single sacrament, it remained problematical to distinguish one from the other objectively, for the gift of the Holy Spirit which should be distinctive of confirmation is also a proper effect of baptism. The affirmation that confirmation gives the fullness of the Spirit is not sufficient in itself to demonstrate the distinction between the two sacraments.

Confirmation has been spoken of as the sacrament of Christian maturity and the apostolate, but even these characteristics which should more directly lead to the thought of the ecclesial function of confirmation came to be looked upon in a perspective of subjective sanctification. And it was often precisely the consideration that the confirmed should be a mature member of the faithful and one ready for the apostolate which led to the idea that confirmation should be conferred at a more advanced age.[5]

Basically, since the effects of confirmation were practically reduced to the increase of grace already acquired in baptism, it was easy to conclude that confirmation—non-determinative as

[4] For the discussions that arose after the affirmations of G. Dix, see A. Caprioli, "Rassegna di Teologia sul sacramento della cresima," in *Scuola Catt. Suppl. Bibl.* 91 (1963), pp. 131-46.

[5] When confirmation was spoken of as the sacrament of the apostolate, an ecclesial perspective was basically involved, but there was equivocation concerning the nature of the apostolate which came to be understood predominantly as a direct and explicit action of proselytism both within and without the Church.

far as the purposes of eternal salvation were concerned—could be conferred even a long time after baptism. But the most deleterious consequences of considering the sacramental effects solely on the subjective level was that of making it practically impossible to grasp the logical connection linking the development of sacramental action, thus leading to the view that a certain order of succession is of no consequence. The developments of the theology of the sacraments and present-day ecclesiology are on the way to enabling us to surpass these perspectives.

If we admit that the sacraments structure the Church as the mystery of salvation and worship, it is no longer possible to regard them solely as goods to be distributed in accord with the needs of the faithful. This is true especially of the three sacraments which confer a character. If character is what renders perennially visible the sacramental salvific act through which the subject is called to constitute the People of God and to structure it hierarchically as a visible community of salvation and worship, it is logical that the order of development of the sacramental act be derived from the nature of the Church even before it is derived from the necessities of the faithful.[6]

However, in order to grasp the significance of this affirmation we must take note of the confirmation-eucharist relation in addition to the baptism-confirmation relation. The eucharistic celebration is the culminating moment in which the mystery of the Church is realized. In the actual historical order—while awaiting the eschatological realization—the Church can never find a more efficacious and fuller realization than that which takes place in the celebration of the eucharist. This is why we must emphasize the incongruity of conferring confirmation after one has already been called to live the mystery itself in its greatest realization.[7]

[6] E. Ruffini, "Character as a Concrete Visible Element of the Sacrament in Relation to the Church," in *Concilium* 31 (1968), pp. 101-14. We believe this observation is ultimately confirmed by what is said by J. Dournes, "Why Are There Seven Sacraments?" in *Concilium* 31 (1968), p. 79, note 22.

[7] P. Massi, "Confermazione e partecipazione all'Eucaristia," in *La confermazione e l'iniziazione cristiana* (Turin, 1967), pp. 52-68.

For some, the fact that the eucharist can be received more than once eliminates all incongruity,[8] but such affirmations are possible only if one continues to consider the sacraments— including the eucharist—exclusively in terms of a subjective sanctification. In its sacrificial aspect (of Christ and the Church) and consequently in its cultual dimension, the eucharist is not an attempt for the realization of the Church which must be repeated in order to be successful. The repetition of the eucharistic act stems from the fact that the Church is a mystery which is actuated on the historical order and thus has need of being prolonged in time.

Naturally, the eucharist is also a sacrament of sanctification and it is logical that in its repetition the faithful should find a means of spiritual progress. In this sense we can also understand that a non-confirmed person is admitted to the eucharist, and it is on this plane that we can make legitimate a practice which perdures everywhere and from years back. But we must ask ourselves if it is worthwhile to retain a practice in which the distinction between the eucharist as a sacrifice and as a sacrament is inadvertently heightened when all efforts are presently being directed toward uniting the sacramental and sacrificial dimensions of the eucharist.

We have insisted on stressing the incongruity of conferring confirmation after the eucharist because the cycle—baptism, confirmation, eucharist—constitutes the complete trajectory of Christian initiation. But this is not only incongruity; there are others which—already present in actual practice—would ultimately be noticed if the age of confirmation were to be indiscriminately pushed back.[9]

[8] G. Negri, "A proposito dell'età della cresima," in *La confermazione* (Turin, 1967), pp. 69-75; E. Alberich, "Pastorale giovanile e sacramenti," in *Orientamenti Pedagogici* 14 (1967), pp. 1324-63.

[9] "Can we still reasonably speak about sacraments of Christian initiation when these are delayed to such a point that to receive them one must first be admitted to the sacrament of penance?": A. Nocent-S. Marsili, "Problemi contemporanei della iniziazione cristiana," in *La confermazione* (Turin, 1967), p. 34.

Age of Confirmation or Age of Initiation?

To resolve the question of the age of confirmation even at the cost of altering the cycle of Christian initiation signifies the acceptance of a pastoral method divorced from theology and weak in its bases. If the conditions of our age require the serious confrontation of a problem of age, it should be done in terms of initiation taken as a whole. If, for example, we do not wish to make the age of first communion a subject of discussion, we will need to be logical and regulate the age of confirmation accordingly.

However, in our day a much more radical problem is becoming evident. In a society so profoundly de-Christianized we must ask whether the practice of conferring baptism on infants should not be revised.[10] It may be that our situation requires so radical a revision, and, naturally, if the age of baptism is pushed back, the lateness of confirmation is completely discounted. But even a rethinking in this sense must take account of all the theological principles that may be involved.

It has been observed that in order not to reduce the sacramental action to a magical activity, the subject must of necessity take part in it with a lively faith. It is true that in the exaggerated affirmation of the objective efficacy of the sacraments, there is danger of magic, but the thesis which unduly emphasizes the importance of human activity involves just as much danger. Indeed, the most traditional form of magic consists precisely in attributing to human activity the capacity to condition the divine action, even to the extent of being able to dominate it.

Contemporary theology has justly regained the theocentric dimension of the sacraments; they are the means by which God comes to us even before they are the means by which we go to him. The actual economy of salvation, which includes the sacraments, provides for human collaboration but continues to remain

[10] Cf. the note of the French Episcopate, *Docum. Cath.* 63 (1966), p. 457; P. Peuchmaurd, "Qui faut-il baptiser," in *Parole et Mission* 28 (1965).

an economy in which the gratuity of the divine salvific action is predominant.

Is it really certain that the kingdom of God will be better structured as a visible community of salvation by reducing it to a communion of adults only—even though they be convinced adults? Is this really a biblical perspective?

Some reforms are necessary to reinvest Christian initiation with a more logical development, but since it is the sacramental life itself which must work for its own completion,[11] we hold that the age of discretion is, along normal lines, the most suitable for the conferral of confirmation. To resolve the undeniable difficulties of our de-Christianized age, we believe that other paths should be chosen which may be more difficult but less illusory.

[11] P. Ranvez, "Les sacrements de l'initiation chrétienne et l'âge de la première communion," in *Lumen Vitae* 19 (1964), pp. 617-34; E. Ruffini, "L'età della cresima nel pensiero teologico contemporaneo," in *Scuola Catt.* 95 (1967), pp. 62-79.

Petrus Huizing, S.J./*Nijmegen, Netherlands*

The Indissolubility of Marriage and Church Order

A symposium on "The Bond of Matrimony" was held at Notre Dame University, October 15-18, 1967, under the auspices of the Canon Law Society of America and presided over by William W. Bassett, professor at the Faculty of Canon Law in the Catholic University of America. It was meant to be a contribution to the revision of the Church order of marriage. This was indeed achieved in a significant degree, as is clear when one compares the understanding of the problems and the conclusions reached by the symposium with the regulations about the indissolubility of marriage as they appear in the Code of Canon Law of Whitsun, 1918.

These regulations can be summarized as follows. In principle every marriage is indissoluble. The sacramental character of the marriage between two baptized partners reinforces this indissolubility. It is totally impossible for the partners to break the bond themselves. This is called the intrinsic indissolubility which allows of no exceptions. The sacramental marriage bond between two baptized partners, when consummated (*matrimonium ratum et consummatum*), cannot be set aside by ecclesiastical authority. This is called the extrinsic indissolubility. Any marriage which is not sacramental, or does not exist between two baptized partners, and/or is not consummated, can be dissolved by the Church in principle and under certain conditions.

Various possibilities of dissolution can be distinguished. The oldest case is that of a marriage between two partners who are not baptized. This is referred to in 1 Corinthians 7, 12-16, and is designated by the name of "Pauline privilege". The conditions here are that one of the partners is baptized after the marriage and the other does not wish to continue on this basis or to accept it peacefully. A subsequent Christian marriage then dissolves the first one.

The second case dates from the Middle Ages. It concerns a marriage that is not consummated. The conditions in this case are that at least one of the partners wants to break off the marriage and the lack of consummation is established with moral certainty. Another possibility, that of an unconsummated marriage being dissolved by the solemn religious profession of at least one of the partners, is obviously very rare in practice.

The third case is the dissolution of a marriage between two non-Catholics, of whom one is baptized, the other not. The first known application of this case only dates from 1924. Today it is frequent. The conditions are that one partner joins the Catholic Church and marital life can no longer be continued. The impossibility of continuing the marital life must not be attributable to the converted partner, at least not at the time when the dissolution is applied for and granted. This dissolution is also pronounced by the pope personally.

The fourth case, still more recent, is that of the dissolution of a marriage between a Catholic and a non-baptized partner after dispensation from the impediment of mixed marriage. The conditions in this case are that the marriage has irremediably broken down and that that impossibility of mending it cannot be blamed on the Catholic partner at the time of the application and its approval.

Finally, the pope today also grants the dissolution of a marriage between two non-Catholics, one of whom is certainly not baptized and neither partner a member of the Catholic Church. The conditions are here that in fact the marriage has already broken down and that the dissolution is necessary in order to enable one of the partners to contract a new marriage with a Catholic partner.

These ecclesiastical regulations are based on two principles. The first is Christ's statement that man may not separate what God has united, and this applies to all marriages without exception. The second is the power to bind and to loose given by Christ to Peter and his successors, and this as Christ's delegates, and not in virtue of some purely human competence. Theologians and canonists generally took it for granted that the power to dissolve did not extend to sacramentally consummated marriages. In 1936 O'Connor maintained that the indissolubility of the marriage in the New Testament referred exclusively to intrinsic indissolubility alone, that the papal competence to dissolve extended *per se* also to the dissolution of sacramentally consummated marriages, but that the Church had definitely limited herself to the non-exercise of this power.[1] In 1967 Pospishil launched a plea that this power to dissolve should also be applied to sacramentally consummated marriages.[2]

The first question put to the participants of the symposium above mentioned was that of the New Testament basis of this Church order of marriage.[3] It was introduced by Crossan who reached the following conclusions. The New Testament teaching on divorce and remarriage implies two aspects. The first is the apodictic and general condemnation of divorce and remarriage. This is the common teaching of the Synoptics and Paul. All put it forward as originating in Christ's own teaching. The second concerns the exceptions mentioned in Matthew 5, 32; 19, 9 and in 1 Corinthians 7, 12-16. Crossan interprets the well-known phrases of Matthew, "except in the case of *porneia*" (unchastity) as added by Matthew himself. The Christian community which he represented was faced with the concrete problem of pagans who were married against the laws of Leviticus 18, and who wanted to be baptized and accepted in the fellowship of the Judaeo-

[1] W. O'Connor, "The Indissolubility of a Ratified, Consummated Marriage," in *Eph. Theol. Lov.* 13 (1936), pp. 692-722.

[2] V. Pospishil, *Divorce and Remarriage* (London, 1967).

[3] D. Crossan, *Divorce and Remarriage in the New Testament* (ms).

Christians. They were allowed divorce and remarriage, or were even advised to divorce. Paul had another problem to cope with. There were Christians whose Gentile partners no longer wanted to cohabit with them in peace and harmony after their baptism. He, too, allowed divorce and remarriage.

How then did the first Christians interpret Jesus' apodictic condemnation of divorce and remarriage? The best way to understand this categorical imperative of Jesus is to see it in the context of Matthew 5, 13-32, namely, the Sermon on the Mount. This also contains the categorical prohibitions of swearing and resisting injustice. But these categorical prohibitions are made relative by the necessity to control deceit and aggressive violence in serious situations. Divorce, like lies and wars, is a tragic human failure. But when these things happen irretrievably, then the apodictic condemnation of their possibility does not tell us how to deal with them in their reality. Today, too, Christian communities are faced with situations where they have to reconcile Jesus' general condemnation with God's call to a life in peace. The categorical imperative of Jesus cannot be used as an absolute law in all cases, but only as an ideal contained in the proclamation. The New Testament itself mentions two exceptions in the widening experience of life. Unfortunately, far more exceptions will have to be made; in far more cases divorce and remarriage will have to be accepted, however sadly, as facts of inevitable human weakness and the inability to live together before Christ will be all in all.

The conclusions reached in this paper agree with those contained in B. Häring's study on the normative value of the Sermon on the Mount.[4] This would have consequences with regard to the still valid canonical norm which excludes the dissolution of a sacramentally consummated marriage. The canon then could not be directly based on a positive law laid down by Christ. In certain social circumstances Canon Law can, of course, be a means toward the realization of the ideal of the Gospel. This would then

[4] B. Häring, "The Normative Value of the Sermon on the Mount," in *Cath. Bibl. Quart.* 29 (1967), pp. 375-85.

be the meaning of the declaration of the Council of Trent that the Church does not err when, in accordance with the Gospel, she teaches and has taught that the sacramentally consummated marriage cannot be dissolved. In this case, however, the canonical regulation would not be identical with Christ's pronouncement. It remains then unthinkable for the Church in principle to deny the ideal of marriage as an indissoluble bond and as a mandate contained in the Gospel, but it would not be unthinkable in principle that, in certain cases of an irreparable breakdown, Canon Law recognizes the dissolution of the marriage.

It is well known that in the earlier centuries and the first half of the Middle Ages not all Fathers and councils and popes saw the indissolubility of Christian marriage as an established fact.[5] A careful analysis of the imperial legislation from Constantine in 331 to Justinian in 566 shows that this legislation is not aware of the principle of absolute indissolubility.[6] It is based rather on the Platonic principle of Novella 22 of the Code of Justinian: "Of all the things that happen among men, all that is bound can be unbound." Yet, the conviction of Jerome, Ambrose and Augustine that remarriage is invalid as long as the other partner is alive was certainly known and shared by a number of others. The fact that the Christian emperors did not follow this opinion proves that there was no unanimity as yet on this point. Between 331 and 566 Christians could hold in good faith that a marriage could be dissolved without incurring the charge of heresy. This does not, of course, warrant any conclusions for later ages.

The Eastern theological tradition concerning divorce and remarriage rests on its own special understanding of sacramentality.[7] "Sacraments" or *mysterion* implies transformation, a transition from old to new, and therefore also has an eschatological implication. The sacraments manifest within this world the reality of the world to come, and they communicate this reality. The finality of the content of marriage for those baptized in

[5] Pospishil, *op. cit.*, gives the relevant texts with commentary.
[6] J. Noonan, *Novel 22*.
[7] A. Schmemann, *The Indissolubility of Marriage: The Theological Tradition of the East* (ms).

Christ is no longer merely earthly happiness but the *martyrion*, the witness to God's kingdom. It receives the strength to serve Christ and has a special function in the ecclesial community. This marriage transcends the categories of binding and loosing. It belongs to ecclesiology and eschatology, the theology of "glory". The real antinomy of the "impossible" demands included in the deification of man and the infinite compassion of the God incarnate who took man's sins upon himself are essential to the Eastern tradition. The Church proclaims the glory of marriage in the baptized person, and at the same time recognizes man's existential ambiguity as one of the main sources of tension between good and evil, between the new Adam and the old. The Church recognizes marriage also as inexorably rooted in the tragedy of original sin.

The point here is not so much a matter of compromise, or tolerance, or *oikonomia*. Marriage *is* indissoluble, and yet *is* also constantly broken through sin, ignorance, passion, selfishness, lack of faith and lack of love. The Church recognizes the dissolution of a marriage but does not dissolve it. She merely recognizes the fact that here and now, in this concrete situation, the marriage has broken down, is finished. A second marriage, compassionately allowed by the Church, is no longer the *mysterion*, the "sacrament", which the first was. Nor does it exclude the partners from the community. The essence of Eastern teaching on marriage lies in this apparently paradoxical tension between its relationship to Christ and his kingdom—and hence the inner solidity of the marriage—and its being rooted in human weakness and sinfulness—and hence its liability to break down.

The theoretical arguments usually adduced to prove the indissolubility of marriage are based on the sacramental character, the interest of the children and the common good. Professor Dupré and his wife have made a study of these arguments.[8] The sacramental character is not the decisive factor in this indissolubility. It merely confirms the general positive divine law. In-

---

[8] L. and C. Dupré, *The Indissolubility of Christian Marriage and the Common Good* (ms).

asmuch as this law is not clear, only the "natural" arguments can be decisive. Is it in the interest of the children to preserve a marriage when the personal bond between the parents has been broken? The prevention of divorce does not prevent broken homes or homes that have in fact been abandoned by father or mother. The impossibility to marry again may also mean that the child will be deprived of adequate material support, and of what it perhaps needs most, a second father or mother.

In the past the common good or social order used to be understood as the maximum of stability and the minimum of change. In a primitive community legal order tends toward a powerful protection of institutions. But in a developed community where the institutions are sufficiently established, legal order leaves more scope for the rights of the person. Has the Church not reached a stage of maturity where the institution of marriage is established firmly enough? Does Church law with regard to divorce sufficiently reflect that shift from the institutional to the personal aspects of marriage which has taken place in modern society? Church law still presupposes the validity of marriage in its institutional aspect as long as the contrary—the personal freedom of the partners—is not proven with morally certain arguments. Could this presumption not be turned round so that the freedom of exercise of personal rights is presumed unless the validity of the institutional aspect is morally certain? What kind of value is there in the inalienable right to a full marital development if the marital relationship remains unalterably subordinate to the existing agreement, however feeble the grounds on which this agreement rests? For centuries the Church has recognized in the Pauline privilege the right of the person to the full practice of his faith as prior to the institutional aspect of marriage. Why cannot constant adultery, though even more inwardly destructive of the marriage bond than dissimilarity of faith, be accepted as a ground for divorce?

One of the key issues in the matter of indissolubility concerns the content of a marriage that has irretrievably lost every marital relationship between the partners. Is the mere "protraction" of a marriage the main norm for a "lasting" and "stable" marriage? According to this norm many "defective" marriages could be really "stable" and "good". Dr. Higgins has dealt with this question from the psychiatric point of view with every caution and in great detail.[9] His conclusions point to the importance of a proper education for marriage, of marriage counseling that is both more widely available and more expert in every way, and of an understanding of neurotic influences on marriage, accompanied by the need for available and adequate treatment. But even with all this, one has to face the fact that the only solution for some marriages is their dissolution.

A sociological investigation of marriage and family in the United States has established that since urbanization and the two world wars there has been an increase in both liberalization and secularization.[10] Marriage is seen as a civil rather than as a sacramental contract, and is therefore liable to dissolution under certain circumstances. Panic about the increasing divorce rate is a mistake. Over the last twenty years the rate has not increased, nor can such an increase be foreseen. It is true that divorce is more generally and openly accepted. The greater number of women who go out to work has changed the marital situation and the way of bringing up the children. Intimate relations, both inside and outside marriage, are more freely accepted, partly because of the development of the "pill", and partly because sexuality is seen as personal identification and not only as a matter of procreation. Marriages are more likely to be stable according to the higher level of income, education and work of the partners. Early marriages—more or less trial marriages—increase the number of divorces followed by a speedy remarriage. More than half the divorced parents have children. Divorce is preferred to the disadvantages implied in the education by one of the parents or by two incompatible parents. The harm done to the child—not by divorce, but by marital conflicts—is

[9] J. Higgins, *The Matrimonial Bond: A Critique from Clinical Psychiatry* (ms).

[10] M. Sussman, *The Family in the 1960's: Facts, Fictions, Problems, Prospects and Institutional Linkages* (ms).

taken much more seriously, even when efforts are made to hide these conflicts from the children.

Within the framework of existing Canon Law about marriage, Dailey pleads for the annulment of marriages on the ground of a sociopathic (psychopathic) condition existing at the time when the marriage is contracted and making the patient unable to fulfill the marital duties.[11] No one can validly accept obligations which he cannot fulfill because of a deficiency in himself, existing at the time when he undertakes these obligations. One of the essential conditions of contracts in general is that the object of the contract must be possible. The sociopath suffers from inadequate will power and emotional disturbances, and also from inadequate judgment. He is incapable of judging himself objectively. There are also cases of homosexuals where afterward it becomes clear that they could not be expected to be able to fulfill their marital duties in a human way for a lengthy period. If this incapacity existed at the time when the marriage was concluded and the present condition of the homosexual is a sort of continuation of that incapacity, one may take it that he or she could not validly undertake the duties of a married person.

In the present canonical system such cases of sociopathy and homosexuality would fall under the heading of marriages that are "null and void". In the category of "indissoluble marriages" the question arises whether the mere ritual undergoing of baptism can really be taken as decisive for the indissolubility of marriage. It happens that a previous marriage cannot be undone if both partners were baptized even though one or even both of them did not know of this baptism and never had any personal contact with any religion whatsoever. If such a marriage is held to be absolutely indissoluble, do we not attribute to the rite of baptism a kind of spiritually automatic effect? The answer to this may perhaps be found in 1 Corinthians 7, 12-16. Absolute indissolubility is linked with the fact that the man and woman are both Christians. The male Christian is a "brother", the female

[11] R. Dailey, *The Marriage of Christians—Valid Sacrament, Valid Contract?* (ms).

Christian a "sister". They are people who are baptized in the faith and have been incorporated in the community of the believers. The "two in one flesh" means—apart from and above the physical consummation of the marriage—a shared life which is explicitly related to the mystery of Christ and his Church in the Christian marriage. The relation becomes explicit through baptism *and* through the visible incorporation into the Christian community. If one of these two factors is lacking, at least in the sense that one of them has never taken place, then marriage cannot have this explicit relationship, and is the same as the "natural" marriage, good in itself, and a non-explicit sign of Christ's union with his Church, but not absolutely indissoluble.

The discussions of the symposium led to the following conclusions, among others: existential indissolubility is of paramount importance and cannot be replaced by a juridical concept of indissolubility; social facts and influences require a new reflection on the Church's teaching about indissolubility; here Scripture does not provide an adequate argument for the current interpretation of this teaching, nor do the Fathers, tradition or the pronouncements of the magisterium; the content of the sacramental character of marriage and its connection with indissolubility are not clear; the present Canon Law concerning marriage, and particularly indissolubility, is not logical and coherent enough to help us.

Personally I am inclined to think that a consistent reflection on the canonical tradition *is* able to help us. Jurisprudence has already disentangled the principle that marriage is made by the contract (*consensus facit matrimonium*) from many presumptions. It can still be formulated more exactly. And this holds also for a second basic principle: the sacrament and the marital agreement of baptized persons are identical. These principles occur in Canons 1012 and 1081, § 1.

To be "married in Christ"— as the fulfillment of his Word: "What God has united no man shall separate"—therefore does *not* mean the cohabitation of a man and a woman kept together by social pressure or by a law, even an ecclesiastical one. It is not a commission given to Peter and the apostles to keep married people together by disciplinary measures. Christ's words mean first of all an invitation and commission addressed to married partners who believe in his redemption to love one another as redeemed persons, and with a love which seeks to be irrevocable, and will never be withdrawn. It is the partners themselves who are baptized in Christ and of whom it is asked and expected that they embody in their contract the dimensions of redeemed love with all this implies, such as the "carrying of one another's burden", the forgiving seventy times seven times and the giving of one's life for the other. The "contract"—i.e., the concluding of a marriage in a form accepted by the ecclesial community—is a sacramental sign as a visible event only when it is, and means to be, the expression of this total and unconditional giving of oneself. The "sacrament" is only present in its full operative reality when the man and the woman express in their lives this mutual gift. This reality can also exist between two people who have never been baptized—or, to put it in a technical way, as a *votum sacramenti*, the implied wish for the sacrament.

Indissolubility, as a datum of the Christian faith, is therefore not a law imposed from without, certainly not as a natural law, or as a "positive divine law", or as an "ontological" datum. It is the offer of the redemption of love between man and woman from the oppression of human selfishness and shortsightedness, and the acceptance of this redemption. I have been told frequently that this kind of indissolubility only occurs, and only can occur, in the case of a very small elite. My reply is that anyone with a little experience in these matters knows of numerous partners in marriage who may probably be unable to put it in these words but who experience in themselves the realization that they are indissolubly united. They also realize that this inner indissolubility has its roots somewhere in their faith and in their clinging to Christ.

This evangelical indissolubility exists in the married partners themselves. Consciously or unconsciously it is built up by them in the power of Christ's redemption. No more than marriage itself can it be built up by anyone else, not even by Church law. And where this kind of indissolubility exists, no one can undo it, not even ecclesiastical authority. I am therefore strongly inclined to accept that the dissolutions declared by Church authority, mentioned at the beginning of this article, are simply situations where historical experience has taught the community that this evangelical indissolubility simply did not exist. The teaching that the ecclesiastical authority, or the pope as the vicar of Christ, would have received the power to dissolve certain marriages would therefore have to be developed in depth. As long as two married partners, baptized or not, do not want to break the bond that unites them, no authority whatever, not even the Church, has any competence to impose it. Authority can only "dissolve" when in fact the partners themselves have already broken the bond. Just as the community can indeed recognize a marriage, but not make it, so can the community recognize the dissolution of a marriage, but not create it.

In the aforementioned dissolutions it is in the marriage situation itself that the evangelical indissolubility is lacking because the partners themselves have never "made" it. They are therefore not inwardly bound to this kind of indissolubility. Since marriage is essentially related to the community, the freedom to separate is not a merely personal matter but rightly demands recognition by the community.

Those who can accept this view will also understand that the simple undergoing of the baptismal rite, the outward canonically valid marriage and the fact of physical consummation by no means guarantee that this evangelical indissolubility between the partners exists in fact, and that they are therefore irrevocably bound to it. In this sense the "sacramental and consummated" marriage is not absolutely indissoluble, at least not in virtue of an absolutely binding scriptural norm. It is possible that this evangelical indissolubility does not exist, or does not yet exist, even between two baptized partners who are married in a form recognized by the Church and who show no observable ground for nullity in terms of present Canon Law. One may perhaps even go so far as to maintain that when such a marriage is irremediably broken down, this is a strong indication that this indissolubility never existed. Therefore the canonical grounds for nullity, fixed and formulated through the historical experience of the ecclesial community—namely the "deficient consent" in its various forms—must be investigated in depth and reduced to their real cause. This cause will then be seen to coincide with the real reason why certain marriages can be "dissolved" by the ecclesiastical authorities.

This attempt at rethinking the teaching on indissolubility is given here for what it is worth. It is obvious that this kind of indissolubility and this kind of sacramentality are far more difficult to formulate in juridical terms than as presented in Canon Law. It is equally obvious that there would be far-reaching consequences in our time for the way in which Church order deals with marriage. I am in any case convinced that the serious and generally expert labor undertaken under the auspices of the Canon Law Society of America inescapably forces us to rethink the teaching on indissolubility. The method pursued in this symposium might point the way for this process.

Ladislas Örsy, S.J./*New York, N.Y.*

Mixed Marriage

The Catholic Church today is like a human person who has received a new insight but has not had time as yet to put it into practice. Vatican Council II has brought about a new vision, but the Church has had no possibility as yet to draw all the practical implications. Such a situation is particularly evident in the matter of mixed marriages. A new theological understanding is emerging concerning the existing unity of all Christians, a unity more important than their differences. Yet the legislation of the Church for mixed marriages is mainly based on a pre-conciliar theology that centered on the differences. No wonder tension is in the air. To resolve it we need new laws born from a new vision. The aim of this article is to propose these new laws. To achieve this aim, the present legal situation will be described; then it will be contrasted with the new theological vision arising from Vatican Council II; finally, practical suggestions will be offered as to how the law could follow the doctrine.

I

THE PRESENT LEGAL SITUATION

At the time when this article is being written the legal situation concerning mixed marriages is in a process of development. The provisions of the Code still predominate, although the Instruction promulgated (with the special authority of Paul VI) by the Congregation for the Doctrine of Faith on March 18, 1966 introduced some changes. The Episcopal Synod of 1967 found the topic on its agenda and the bishops voted eight propositions in view of the reform of the law.

In the Code there is a prohibition in the form of an impediment against the marriage of a Catholic with a non-Catholic Christian. Such a marriage cannot be contracted lawfully unless a dispensation is granted by the bishop. If a dispensation is not asked for, or asked for but not granted, the parties would still be able to contract a *valid* marriage in theory, although not so in practice. No pastor or bishop would assist at the marriage, and without the presence of either of these, no valid marriage could be contracted. Hence there is no practical possibility for any Catholic to contract a mixed marriage validly without dispensation.

The Code requires that the bishop granting the necessary dispensation must be satisfied that there is moral certainty that the faith of the Catholic party is not in danger and that all the children will be educated in the Catholic faith. This moral certainty is usually proved by the so-called *cautiones* or promises in various forms: in writing signed by both parties, or verbally, perhaps confirmed by an oath, or, rarely, by circumstantial evidence without any explicit declaration.

No one would really quarrel with the provision that the faith of the Catholic party should not be endangered. Nor should the faith of the non-Catholic party be endangered. But many non-Catholics resent deeply the law that all the children have to be educated in the Catholic religion. After all, the children are *their* children too.

The Instruction of March 18, 1966 retained the outlook of the Code but introduced some changes that are of importance. If the non-Catholic party cannot sign the promises without hurting his own conscience, or if he refuses to contract the marriage according to the Catholic form, the case should be referred to the Holy See. The Instruction does not say in what way the Holy See will provide in these cases. However, some jurisprudence is already emerging, and it seems that the Congregation is prepared to grant a dispensation from the impediment of mixed religion provided the Catholic party states that he is aware of his duty to educate the children in the Catholic faith and promises to do all that he can in the circumstances to fulfill his duty. Also, evidence is required to show that the non-Catholic party knows about the obligations of his Catholic partner. On rare occasions, it appears that a dispensation from the Catholic form of marriage is granted. If this presentation of a new jurisprudence is correct (it cannot be confirmed from any public document) there is no doubt that the Instruction marks the beginning of a new departure. No proof of moral certainty is required that the children will be educated in the Catholic faith, but rather some evidence about the determination of the Catholic party to do his duty as best he can. No promise is required from the non-Catholic.

The whole issue of mixed marriages was laid before the Synod of bishops in the fall of 1967. From the discussion, different trends of opinions emerged, and they became crystallized in a number of propositions that obtained varying majorities of votes. A sizable majority of the Synodal fathers requested that the terms "mixed marriage", "impediment" and "dispensation" should remain part of our legal terminology. More than two-thirds of them thought that the condition for dispensation from the impediment should be the moral certainty that the Catholic party is not in danger of losing his faith and that he is prepared to do all he can to baptize and educate the children in the Catholic faith. A lesser number of them, but still a majority, held that the non-Catholic party should be fully informed about the duty of the Catholic and also should be willing *not* to put any obstacle to the Catholic baptism and education of the children. Again a large majority were of the opinion that the present structure of the impediment should be retained as well as the duty to contract a mixed marriage in the Catholic canonical form. However, they suggested that the bishop should have power to dispense from this form.

From the opinion of the members of the Synod, three important points emerge:

1. Certainty is required about the present intention of the

Catholic party, not about the future event of the children's education.

2. The non-Catholic party should not be asked to promise the Catholic education of children but to give evidence in some way that he will not oppose it.

3. The right to dispense from the canonical form should be reserved to the bishop and not to the Holy See.

These points are definite steps toward greater understanding. The power to be given to the bishop is far reaching. If given, it is likely that it will be interpreted and used in a more or less uniform way by the members of the same episcopal conference. Of course, the suggestions of the Synod are not laws. However, they foretell the way future legislation is likely to go.

II

THE PRESENT THEOLOGICAL SITUATION

The essence of marriage is that it is a union, a communion of two persons, a life-event in which they reveal themselves to each other and in which God reveals himself to them. There is stability in it and there is movement in it. The theological problem in the mixed marriage is that the communion between the husband and wife is not full. When they reveal themselves to each other, it is a revelation lacking full communion in faith; when they receive God's revelation, they do not understand it in the same way. They are *one* in marriage, but divided in faith and ecclesial communion. The tragedy of the division of the Christians is manifested in a most dramatic way at the heart of the family.

To this problem there is just one perfect solution: the reunion of Christians. As long as we are divided there are only imperfect solutions. At present the question is how the least imperfect solution can be found that serves the theological exigencies of the welfare of the child, the conscience of the Catholic and the non-Catholic, and the cause of the unity of the Church.

The good of the child postulates that he should be received from an early age into a living Christian community. There faith in Christ and the way of life according to the Gospel are communicated to him in an existential way. This experience of Christian community is the most that Christian parents can give to their children—even if the parents are not of the same denomination.

To say that parents should not decide the religion of the child, but let him choose when he has reached the age to make a rational decision, is an overrationalistic approach with little sense for real human situations. To do so would deprive the child of the vital experience of a Christian community. It would delay the choice of religion until the child has the accumulated knowledge to make a decision. Even then the existential knowledge of any type of Christianity so necessary for such a choice would be lacking. It would not serve the welfare of the child if he were deprived of the experience of Christian living in a community.

Further, it is said sometimes that children born from mixed marriages should be divided into two religious groups—the boys perhaps following the religion of the father and the girls following the religion of the mother. This solution is presented as just and fair, yet no solution can be further from the generous and warm spirit of true ecumenism than this one. It reflects a cold, calculating and mean spirit. It perpetuates the division of Christians and instills into the children from an early age the necessity of carefully outlined frontiers, not to say barriers, among them. It is not surprising that it was thought out and practiced when Christians of different denominations looked at each other as enemies. Then the armistice line was drawn right in the middle of the family with strict justice and little concern for unity and charity.

The welfare of the child also postulates that nominal solutions should not take the place of real ones. If the Catholic party is a nominal Christian and the non-Catholic is sincerely committed to his own faith, it is difficult to see by what right the religious education of the child should be given to the parent who does not practice his religion.

The Conscience of the Parents

The Church believes that the Catholic parent has both the right and duty to communicate his faith to his child. This communication is not confirmed to verbal instructions. It is the transmission of a way of life, of the joy of sharing a divine gift. This right and duty are not peculiar to persons living in mixed marriages; they are simply the specifications in a mixed marriage situation of the right and duty of every Christian to share the kingdom of God with other human beings. Obviously enough, a parent will want to bring the Good News first to the one who is nearest and dearest to him, to his child. To deny this would not make sense; it would be equivalent to negating the dynamic character of Christianity in the parent. Yet this right and duty exist in the larger context of values. Their exercise will depend on charity and discretion, on the understanding that even God himself reveals himself gradually and with much respect for his own creatures.

A value that should be never lost sight of is the human right to marriage. It is so fundamental that it exists in a Catholic person even when there is no hope of the Catholic education of his future children. This was effectively recognized some time ago in the case of mission lands, and the Instruction of March 18, 1966 reaffirmed it. If in a country where the social, political or religious circumstances make a purely Catholic marriage almost impossible and the Catholic education of children most improbable, the Catholic is still entitled to marry in the way he can. He will have to use wisdom to determine how to communicate his faith to his child. If it will not be through baptism and instruction, it will be perhaps by the example of a life and by silent attraction.

The Church believes that a non-Catholic person of good faith also has the right to communicate his conviction to others. Even if he differs from us on certain points of doctrine, he has the dignity of a Christian person. He has the right to communicate his faith to his own child.

Obviously the faith and freedom of both parents should be respected; they have an equal personal dignity. But it is here that the tragedy of division manifests itself again, for the potential recipient of their divided mind is the child. He is exposed to the experience of the division of Christians even before he can grasp the value of their unity. To respect the conscience of each of the parents is important. Yet the parents have a duty in conscience to give the best Christian experience to the child. Does this mean that it would be better if they agreed that all the children will be educated in one and the same religion? The conclusion seems inescapable.

The Good of the Community

Marriage is not a purely private affair; it has social implications. All human communities, be they tribes, nations or the whole community of men, are interested in the social impact of family life. No wonder; healthy families are the good foundation for any larger community. It is the right and the duty of the community to provide laws that help the development of this family life, laws that foster and protect the good of the child, of the parents and of the community itself. The Catholic Church, too, is a community concerned with the welfare, including the religious welfare, of the family. She, too, promulgates laws to protect and help the family. In making such laws she cannot consider her own interest in a narrow sense; the need of all Christian Churches for unity should be her concern. Marriage laws should also radiate such an understanding and charity that they could be a sign for non-believers of the reign of God among men.

III

FUTURE LEGISLATION

From the contrast between the currently valid legislation and the new theological vision a clear need for new laws arises. The

fathers of the Synod of 1967 saw this need and made some practical suggestions. No doubt the next official step will be the adop-
tion of their propositions. Yet these propositions were not
intended as final solutions but as reasonable steps toward establishing increasing harmony and unity among Christian Churches.
Other steps will have to follow. It is legitimate to ask what they
should be.

General Principles of Legislation

Before suggesting any specific law, let us consider the theological and practical principles that should inspire the new
legislation.

1. The problem of mixed marriages should be lifted out of
any type of interconfessional rivalry. The greatest problem of
Christianity today is not that of mixed marriages. It may be the
most painful one, but it is not the greatest one. The greatest
problem is now to bring the light of the Gospel to those who do
not experience it. Even in connection with marriage, the real
problem is how to uphold the Christian dignity of marriage, a
common concern to all Christians. For such great goals Christians should unite. To neglect a common challenge and task for
the sake of the smaller problem of mixed marriages would be an
unbalanced, not to say unchristian, way of conceiving our duties.
We should be united in announcing to the world the wonders of
Christian marriage before we are divided about the form of its
external celebration and the education of children.

2. The general principles of the ecumenical movement should
be applied to the problem of mixed marriages. We should be
intent on increasing our unity and on helping our divisions to
decrease. Therefore, the problem should not be considered in the
context of the needs of one particular Church at the present time,
but our vision should extend to the whole Christian community
of the future, and we should make our laws in such a way that
the cause of unity and the interest of a particular couple are
equally well served. This may imply that in individual cases some
disadvantage follows for one of the Churches. But it implies also

our acknowledgment that the solution we offer to the problem of mixed marriages has a sign value for the whole Christian world; it demonstrates our good will—or the lack of it. Good will is such a great treasure for all Christians that we should do what we can to foster it.

3. No legislation is really good unless it is realistic. No law is realistic unless it is accepted by the majority of the community. In several countries our present legislation on mixed marriages suffered the fate of a rejection by the majority of those for whom it was intended. It has been demonstrated that in Holland, in Germany and in Switzerland, even before Vatican Council II, the great majority of mixed marriages were contracted in disregard of the Church's legislation—i.e., in an *invalid* way. The statistics would be probably worse today. To cling to laws that remain in the books but do not bring fruit in the life of the community is a mistaken concept of jurisprudence.

The same realism postulates that the legislation should take into account not only those who are living a deeply religious life and are committed to their own Church but also those who are weak in their faith and have only a superficial attachment to their own Church. In other words, the legislation should give an opportunity to the strong to deepen their faith and charity and at the same time help the weak to a deeper realization of their commitment to both God and Church. Surely, this is an almost impossible task for a legislator.

4. The legislator should keep in mind the necessarily universal character of his laws. They may not be suitable for every individual situation. Therefore, a certain broadness in the formulation of the laws is required so that the good order and peace of the community may be upheld and at the same time there may be no injustice worked to the individual. But not every moral obligation should be expressed in the form of laws. In fact, whenever it is possible the legislator should refrain from spelling out a legal duty when the existence of a moral duty is clear anyway on broader theological grounds.

5. In the past the Catholic Church unilaterally legislated for

both the Catholic and the non-Catholic party in mixed marriages, and so did many non-Catholic Churches. Good theology and practical wisdom postulate that various Christian Churches should get together and find a solution in common, a solution that should be promulgated perhaps by a joint statement coming from both communities.

6. The laws for mixed marriages should set the human framework for God's revelation to a family suffering from division. They should be tolerant, since our God is supremely tolerant.

A legislation conceived in this spirit is likely to work as a cementing factor among Christians; it is not likely to become a dividing wall among them.

New Laws

Now some specific suggestions can be offered about future legislation.

1. The legal terminology in reference to mixed marriages should be definitely changed. The "impediment of mixed religion" is an expression that does not cover the real situation. Catholic and non-Catholic Christians are one in their baptism, in their faith in God the Father, the Son and the Spirit, and in Jesus Christ their Savior. Therefore, there is a genuine communion between them, even if there are differences. To describe their religious situation as "mixed" is to insinuate the absence of any communion. Perhaps the term "interconfessional marriage" or "inter-Church marriage" would be better.

2. The obvious contradiction between the legal rule which establishes an impediment that in theory never interferes with the validity of marriage and the legal machinery that in practice always invalidates a marriage contracted without dispensation should be removed. Our legislation should be marked by sincerity. Either the impediment should be made absolute (which is, of course, out of the question) or the parties should be given a real opportunity to marry validly even without dispensation. Whether we like it or not, our present approach is considered by many non-Catholics as lacking in honesty. Perhaps the law

should say that in order to contract an interconfessional marriage the Catholic party would have to obtain a "license"—i.e., permission from his bishop. The request for such a license would give an opportunity to the clergy to examine every situation individually and to offer their pastoral care. Perhaps other Churches would like to do the same.

3. Some way should be found that makes it possible for the Catholic Church to accept a non-Catholic celebration of marriage as valid, assuming that the non-Catholic party shares our vision of marriage. This has been done already in connection with the Eastern Orthodox Churches. Negotiations could be initiated with other Christian Churches such as the Anglican or Episcopalian Church, and an agreement could be reached to mutually acknowledge marriages contracted in the presence of a representative of either of the Churches.

4. The Catholic parent has a moral duty to "evangelize" his own children, but this moral duty need not be articulated by the legislator, unless specific and grave reasons compel him to do so. The imposition of the legal duty on the Catholic party to baptize and educate all his children in the Catholic faith is useless unless he is deeply committed to his own faith and Church. If this commitment exists, the legal formalities are superfluous. But if it does not exist, they are mere formalities. Hence good arguments exist for the abolition of legal promises and simultaneously for a more intense preaching of the moral duty.

If a legal obligation is imposed on the Catholic, it should be enough to ask him (a) *to declare* that he is aware of his duty to respect the Church's teaching about the sanctity of marriage and of communicating the Gospel and Christian life to his children; and (b) *to promise* that he intends to fulfill his duties. The promise about the sanctity of marriage would include the duty to work for peace and unity in the family. The promise to communicate his faith to his children would include the intention to educate them in the Catholic religion as far as it can be done without destroying the peace or without interfering with the freedom of his own partner.

Frequently it is stated that such a solution may be convenient for the mixed marriages of persons who are fervent in their faith, but the majority of mixed marriages are in fact concluded between persons weak in their faith. For these a stronger legal expression of their moral duty is needed. This may well be so, and no answer appears other than an honest discussion among the leaders of the Churches admitting the concrete situation and also admitting that for such situations stronger legal safeguards may be necessary. What should be in the mind of the leaders is that the aim should be not exactly a statistical gain to the Church but a gain to our Lord. In concrete circumstances the two may not necessarily coincide.

5. If both parents are good Christians, the right solution seems to be to let them decide about the one religion in which all their children should be educated. Only they are in possession of all the facts. Only they are able to sense and evaluate the many imponderable factors of a marriage. They should make the decision between themselves and God. But both Churches should be interested in helping them not only before the marriage takes place but even more during their married life. The right type of "ecumenical counseling" can lead toward unity.

6. In general, emphasis should be put more on strengthening the faith of our Christians and their commitment than on legal provisions. Training in the love of God and in the love of neighbor among all Christians would serve the cause of Christianity better than any type of law about mixed marriages. Let us keep in mind, however, that a perfect solution does not exist. The best we can hope for is to reach a balance that is most suitable for our days, hoping and praying meanwhile that the day will come when husband and wife and children are one as the Father and Son are one.

Rinaldo Falsini, O.F.M./*Milan, Italy*

Concelebration

This series has already hosted—in 1965—a well-documented article on concelebration.[1] Three years have now passed, and although historico-theological studies have not led to any new and significant results, interesting progress has taken place on the liturgical, pastoral and legislative level.[2]

The new rite prepared by the *Consilium* implementing article 58 of the *Constitution on the Sacred Liturgy* made its appearance on March 7, 1965 and went into effect on the fourteenth of the same month.[3] The ensuing experience has brought about a giant step forward: after serving as the object of study and discussion in the hands of specialists, concelebration of Mass has become a normal fact and has entered into the consciousness of both clergy and Christian people. In this respect, we can justly

[1] H. Manders, C.SS.R., "Concelebration," in *Concilium* 2 (1965), pp. 135-51. We refer the reader to this article for general information on the subject as well as bibliographical material.

[2] Among the books on this point we might mention: L. Della Torre, F. Dell'Oro, R. Falsini, A. Franquesa, V. Joannes, E. Lanne, B. Neunheuser, *Concelebrazione, dottrina e pastorale* (Brescia, 1965), p. 300; A. King, *Concelebration in the Christian Church* (Oxford, 1966), p. 149; P. Jounel, *La Concélébration* (Tournai, 1966), p. 248. Among the numerous articles we might single out: C. Vagaggini, "Il valore teologico e spirituale della messa concelebrata," in *Rivista Liturgica* 52 (1965), pp. 189-219; R. Falsini, "La concelebrazione, il rito da preferire," in *Revista di Pastorale Liturgica* 3 (1965), pp. 435-48; J. H. Hannsens, "De concelebratione Missae in ritibus orientalibus," in *Divinitas* 10 (1966), pp. 482-559; A. M. Roguet, "Pour une théologie de la concélébration," in *Maison-Dieu* 88 (1966), pp. 116-26; B. Neunheuser, "Il Canone nella concelebrazione," in *Rivista Liturgica* 53 (1966), pp. 581-92.

[3] *Ritus servandus in concelebratione missae et ritus communionis sub utraque specie*, editio typica (Typis polyglottis Vaticanis, 1965).

speak of a new ecclesial consciousness, and everyone knows the value of such an affirmation for the life of the Church. Not everything has been resolved, but a new path has been opened and concrete perspectives can already be foreseen and proposed.

The Present Discipline.

Before March 7, 1965, with the exception of the 1,500 cases of experimentation which took place in the preceding months under the supervision of the *Consilium,* we could not properly speak of concelebration in the Latin Church. The Council has stated in n. 57 of the *Constitution on the Sacred Liturgy* that "concelebration . . . has remained in use to this day in the Church, both in the East and in the West", but in n. 58 it felt the need to stipulate that "a new rite of concelebration is to be drawn up", insofar as the one in use in priestly and in episcopal consecration could not seriously be regarded as an acceptable rite, even apart from its somewhat strange origin. Neither theology nor spirituality—much less legislation—harbored any friendly feelings for that infelicitous concelebration.

The point of reference remained ever the private Mass, even though in theory the ideal was the episcopal Mass—but the pomp called for in the *Pontifical* gave it an accentuated note of ostentation, an expression of an outdated and outmoded mentality. Indeed, the *ritus servandus* found in the *Roman Missal* from 1570 to the present was modeled after the read Mass celebrated solely with a minister and did not even provide for the presence and participation of the faithful. Hence, the Latin Church had lost the experience of concelebration, that value which was in use during the first millennium and had been kept in use by the Eastern Church. Not only did the Code of Canon Law fail to propose concelebration; it specifically prohibited it: "Non licet pluribus sacerdotibus concelebrare." [4]

Although the new rite—and we must speak of absolute newness—is unique, it is expressed in various ceremonial forms; it starts from the type of pontifical Mass and deduces the particular

[4] C.I.C., 803.

or minor forms: solemn, sung, read. The discipline of concelebration remains that proposed by the *Constitution on the Sacred
Liturgy*: permission of the ordinary, with the faculty reserved for
every priest to celebrate individually, although limited by the
pastoral needs of the faithful.

With respect to Vatican Council II, however, we note an extension of the cases foreseen: Christmas, Paschal Vigil, occasion
of the pastoral visit. As regards the ritual form, we can see the
obvious influence of the directives of Pius XII and the 1957
declaration of the Holy Office which require for valid concelebration the recitation of the words of consecration by every
concelebrant. According to some, this norm would transform
true concelebration into a collective celebration or co-
celebration.

The fruits of two years' experience with concelebration are
visible in the manner in which the Instruction on the eucharistic
mystery of May 25, 1967 speaks of the problem. In addition to
recalling the doctrinal and spiritual reasons for concelebration—
almost all proposed by the Decree *Ecclesiae sanctae* of March 7,
1965—n. 47 expresses open favor and sympathy with concelebration which is declared to be "an excellent manner of celebration": priests are invited to prefer concelebrated Mass to Mass
privately celebrated, and superiors are urged not only to facili-
tate but also to encourage concelebration, consenting to it even
more than once a day, especially in large communities. However,
the two reservations reappear: every priest is granted the faculty
to celebrate individually and provision must be made for the
pastoral needs of the faithful.

Thus, concelebration no longer appears as an extraordinary
and exceptional rite, but as an ordinary, normal and daily one,
no longer as something prohibited or even merely permitted, but
something favored, preferred and recommended. The situation
has been radically reversed; yet we cannot affirm that all the
consequences have already been drawn. Only an attentive theological reflection and a greater awareness will advance the process so felicitously begun.

Theological Basis and Pastoral Requirements

The problem of concelebration in the period extending from 1945 to Vatican Council II had stirred up general interest chiefly as a solution for the pastoral difficulties arising on occasions of priestly gatherings. The preparatory liturgical commission mentioned these difficulties in the schema of the Constitution, and the central commission accepted them as the sole reason for concelebration during gatherings of the clergy. However, the Council opposed this approach and asked the elimination of the stipulation which would have reduced concelebration to a simple practical expedient; the reason for the existence, or restoration, of concelebration could not depend on an external and negative circumstance. The sole reason adduced by the Council for the justification of concelebration is the unity of the priesthood "appropriately manifested" in such a rite.[5]

The Decree *Ecclesiae sanctae* of March 7, 1965 which promulgated the new rite adds to this the unity of the sacrifice and the unitary action of the entire Christian people. In its turn, the Instruction on the eucharistic mystery of May 25, 1967 proposes another reason of a spiritual nature: the bond of fraternal charity among priests, which has its basis in the common sacred ordination and mission. Then, in cases of priests who are visiting or on pilgrimage, concelebration will acquire—in accord with a very ancient usage—a special sign of hospitality.[6]

The most decisive of the various reasons unquestionably seems to be the unity of the priesthood; indeed, it is concerning this point that difficulties and objections arise, such as the necessity (or less) of reciting the words of consecration and the relation of the concelebrants to the principal celebrant. "Many are the priests"—we read in the Decree *Ecclesiae sanctae*—"who celebrate Mass, and therefore all and each of them are only ministers of Christ who exercises his priesthood through them, and for this reason renders each of them through the sacrament of orders a

---

[5] *Constitution on the Sacred Liturgy,* n. 57.
[6] Instruction on the eucharistic mystery, n. 47.

participant in his own priesthood in a very special manner. Hence, even when they offer the sacrifice individually, all do so in virtue of the same priesthood and act in the person of the high priest to whom it pertains always to consecrate the sacrament of his body and blood, whether through the use of one priest or many at the same time."

This doctrinal point, taken almost verbatim from St. Thomas,[7] is the key to concelebration insofar as it clarifies the figure of the priest: a person who is not absolute and independent but a participant in the unique priesthood of Christ of which he is both sign and prolongation. The multiplicity of priests for the sole benefit of the Church cannot and must not overshadow the unity of participation in this same priesthood; and it is natural that this should reach its most qualified manifestation in that rite which signifies and produces the unity of the body of Christ, that is, the eucharist.

The unity of the priesthood—we should speak of this above all as an *ordo* or *collegium presbyterorum* in which every priest is inserted and made a sharer of the pastoral office of the bishop— necessarily leads to the unity of the sacrifice and the unitary action of the Christian people. Priesthood, eucharist and ecclesial structure are three components or elements of one single reality that refer to one another and contribute to laying the theological foundation of concelebration, which is a collegial and convergent act of all the ministers toward the unique sacrificial act that builds the Christian community.

Therefore, the discourse should not spend itself in the separate analysis of the reasons cited above; it must be extended to a more profound study of the community-hierarchical structure either of the Church or of the individual sacraments. One could answer all the objections raised against concelebration by a still persistent ancient and closed mentality—such as, for example, the question of the fruits of the Mass and the desire of many priests to experience their function integrally; however, concelebration will always remain an object of contention, or rather it will retain its

---

[7] *Summa theologica,* III, 82, art. 3, 2 and 3.

character of external solemnity, until the principles of sacramental theology are revised and the conviction is reached that every sacrament requires the form of concelebration by its very nature.[8]

However, we are equally convinced that the maturation of a valid, organic and theological attitude can be brought about for the most part only through usage. On the other hand, the conciliar accomplishments—among which we might single out, in addition to the new awareness of the *presbyterium*, the basic relation of every priest to his bishop—and the new perspectives of the liturgical reform demand the opportunity for an ever more extended usage of concelebration and the necessity for a deeper and more conscious conviction on the part of the clergy concerning its utility.

It would suffice to recall the fundamental principle expressed in n. 26 of the *Constitution on the Sacred Liturgy* in which the ecclesial, unitary and hierarchical character of every liturgical action is affirmed, and to reread the articles with respect to the individual sacraments concerning their ecclesial aspect. In its turn, n. 41 of the same Constitution recalls that "the preeminent manifestation of the Church consists in the full active participation of all God's holy people in these liturgical celebrations, especially in the same eucharist, in a single prayer, at one altar, at which there presides the bishop surrounded by his college of priests and by his ministers."

Hence, pastoral theology tends—as it were, toward its ideal objective—toward the hierarchical and fraternal gathering around the same altar, and not toward the separation of the assembly into different parts; the latter is also something which the Instruction of May 25, 1967 explicitly urges should be avoided. Two other positions taken by this same document should be noted. Article 42 affirms that "the celebration of the eucharist admirably expresses the public and social nature of the liturgical actions of the Church which is the sacrament of unity,

[8] In this sense Father Roguet is right when he writes (*art. cit.*, p. 116) that "the theology of concelebration is still to be worked out". A fine effort in our eyes is that of V. Joannes in the volume cited above.

that is, a holy people, united and ordered under its bishops".
Article 26, in order to foster the sense of ecclesial community,
proposes a more effective pastoral action together with a reduc-
tion of Masses and a coordinated effort on the part of various
churches.

Thus, fulfillment of pastoral needs does not coincide with the
multiplication of Masses for every group but with truly communitary celebrations. It is a legitimate concern not to deprive
the faithful of Mass, which might be the result of overly frequent
concelebrations, but it is first necessary to define the meaning of
the phrase "pastoral needs". Indeed, we can ask whether it is the
Mass as such which determines the fulfillment of the needs of the
individual faithful and the Church, or whether it is rather the
celebration which is the true expression of the Christian community, present and participating, that both structures and consoli-
dates them.

A more rational method of pastoral action could easily resolve
the apparent harm wrought by concelebration. One would have
to weigh even the value of concelebration in respect to the con-
celebrating priests (sense of brotherhood, charity, consolation,
deeper awareness of the dimension of their priesthood, etc.) or
in respect to the faithful who will acquire a richer and more
intense experience of the eucharist and the Church.[9] The more
expressive the liturgical meaning, the more pastorally valid will
the liturgical action be. Hence, an impartial examination shows
that concelebration is based on solid theological ground and
encounters no obstacle in a well-understood pastoral practice;
rather, it seems in perfect harmony with such practice and is
even demanded by it.

Toward Future Legislation

It will not be easy for the new *jus condendum* to maintain a
position capable of reconciling the old mentality and spirituality
—built on the basis of private Mass without the active participa-

[9] In every case of concelebration it is possible to find a particular
reason and fruit of a pastoral character. Cf. the chapters by L. Della
Torre and R. Falsini in the volume cited above in note 2.

tion of the people—with the new viewpoint which sees its ideal in concelebration, presided over by the bishop, with the united participation of the whole people. The mere repetition of the conciliar reservation regarding the freedom to celebrate individually does not seem sufficient to resolve the contrast once concelebration becomes looked upon as the rite to be preferred.

Logic would dictate that the reverse approach to that of concelebration be verified for private Mass; the latter should take place—especially in communities—only in particular cases. To withdraw from concelebration could give the impression of a weak fraternal spirit, a restricted vision of the eucharist and an inadequate awareness of the communitary value of the Mass in its liturgical expression. Under such circumstances, the reservation becomes curious if not strange; it is true that there are actual historical reasons for its explanation, but it will be ever more incomprehensible to new generations.

Private Mass derives its justification and value from the fact that it retains its social nature as an action of the whole Church. But since the communitary character of the Mass will possess a greater emphasis, the anomaly of a private Mass when concelebration is possible will become ever more glaring. Even if a decision should ultimately be made to allow private Mass only in cases of real difficulty and the impossibility of concelebration, it would not be very desirable—since we are dealing with the creation of a new mentality—to go so far as to impose concelebration; the simple reference to the theological and pastoral reasons for it would suffice.

It would instead be necessary to define the pastoral utility of the individually celebrated Mass for the faithful, insofar as it is proposed as a limitation of concelebration. Obviously, attention should be paid to the phrase "needs of the faithful" which is not equivalent to a simple desire for a Mass for individual interests, but it is clear that such needs are not restricted solely to feast days. Moreover, history teaches that the unity of the Sunday eucharist has suffered eclipse because of pastoral reasons.

Related to the problem of the needs of the faithful is the possibility of bination. Concelebration must not appear merely as an extraordinary and solemn rite. Hence, we do not see the propriety of binating in order to participate at a concelebration, except in the case when a bishop presides, especially on the occasion of a pastoral visit.

The problem of the stipend connected with the Mass intention is more easily soluble. Its legitimacy, acknowledged by Article 10 of the new rite, is deduced from the fact that the offering is not an honorarium for the Mass but a contribution for the subsistence of the priest. The faithful do not receive greater fruits from a private Mass, but it is certain that they look upon it with more affection, and it may be that their offering is intended for a Mass celebrated individually. Therefore, if we were to retain the custom of the offering—which to some appears outdated and inopportune—it would be necessary to give the faithful the real reason for our decision and its significance by means of a disinterested catechesis.

The feared conflicts between the ordinary of the locality and the religious superior—fears voiced during the Council and expressed in Article 57 of the Constitution—have not materialized or at least have been of little consequence. On this point the discipline has evolved in a sense patently in favor of concelebration without particular restrictions or controls, except for the reservation mentioned above. Many ordinaries have granted the permanent faculty to concelebrate. If conflicts of competence between the ordinary of the locality and the religious superior should arise, these would revolve around the pastoral needs of the faithful, and in such a case the judgment of the diocesan ordinary would prevail with the consequent obligation on the part of a religious house to celebrate Mass individually for the needs of the faithful.

The ritual involved brings up a very delicate problem. Although everything has been determined by the new rite, there remains the possibility—if not the requirement, because of a certain suitability—of a revision or development. We are not so much interested in the two marginal questions concerning the number of concelebrants (which in general should not be too great) and the sacred vestments (in this respect, the dispensing of the use of the chasuble by the Instruction *Tres abhinc annos* of May 4, 1967 will be appreciated). But we are very much interested in the grave problem of the necessity of reciting the words of consecration.

Can the solution taken from the new rite be regarded as definitive even in the theological sphere in addition to the disciplinary sphere? Is it really a question of a theological position to be identified with the faith of the Church? Does the evolution verified in reference to the ministerial function of the priest possess a liturgical character, and is it tied to a particular historical situation, or is it perfectly homogeneous to all sacramental evolution? Is the validity of a silent celebration decisively precluded?

The opinions of theologians are not unanimous; in fact, they are openly contradictory. It would therefore be desirable for any new legislation—even while embracing the new ritual dispositions—to refrain from passing a definitive judgment concerning silent concelebration, leaving the theological discussion open. What seems disputable is the statement that in silent concelebrations priests participate in the Mass *more laicorum communicantes* either because communion is identical for all in every case or because this renders an affront to historical truth.

Conclusion

Concelebration has acquired full citizenship rights in the Catholic Church. Less definite is its place in the life and discipline of the Church. The theological questions which still remain should not concern us unduly. In sacramental matters the possession of the Church and her practice have carried an essential weight in theological maturation. Nevertheless, some doctrinal reasons exist for the elaboration of the new legislation in this regard. Experience and reflection must continue. Therefore, it would be helpful if the new legislation did not place obstacles in the way, but rather favored further development.

Teodoro Jiménez-Urresti/*Bilbao, Spain*

The Divine Mission in History and Canonical Missions

V atican Council II, in its examination of the mission of the People of God to reform the Church so that the latter may be better able to fulfill its saving mission, accepts and uses the well-known distinction between divine mission and canonical missions. Previously, the *theory* that the power of jurisdiction descended by an extrasacramentary route from the hands of the pope to the bishops, and from the bishops to the presbyters, claimed that this power was conferred in the canonical mission. Now, the *doctrine* of Vatican Council II teaches that ordination itself confers this power together with those of teaching and sanctifying (cf. *Constitution on the Church*, nn. 20-21). Here the Council resolved a discussion that has lasted for centuries and opened up entire new canonical vistas on pastoral organization. I should like to summarize these here.[1]

[1] Many of the ideas put forward here are developed at greater length in my article of the teaching of Vatican Council II on the episcopal college, in *Comentarios a la Const. sobre la Iglesia* (Madrid, 1966), and in my *Teología del Presbiterado según Vaticano II* (Madrid, 1968). On the historicity of the universal divine mission, see the *Decree on the Church's Missionary Activity*, particularly Chapter I.

I

THE EPISCOPAL COLLEGE—A MISSIONARY

Christ entered into history and fulfilled the redemption of all men in history. Furthermore, he had to apply redemption to each individual through historical means, that is, without transgressing the laws of history. If he had chosen a way outside the course of history, he would have dislocated the logical sequence from his historical redeeming entry into history.

As the *historical* way of applying the redemption he had brought about, he sent out a group of men: the apostolic college. He did not give each apostle a different mission, nor did he confer the mission on each of them separately, but "to all of [them] in common (i.e., as a college) Christ gave his command, thereby imposing on them a common [collegial] duty (*officium*)" (*Constitution on the Church,* n. 23). Therefore, "the growth of the body of Christ is the function (*munus*) of the whole college" (*Decree on the Ministry and Life of Priests,* n. 38), and "the task (*cura*) of proclaiming the Gospel everywhere on earth devolves on the body of pastors" (*Constitution on the Church,* n. 23). As a *mystery,* Christ promised his help and sent his Spirit to the college; as *history,* it is the college, not each member of it, that is infallible, permanent and indefectible. It is *history,* furthermore, that Christ gave Peter the task of keeping the college one and undivided and to move it to action by his example and authority.[2]

Strictly speaking, therefore, there is only one great missionary or bearer of the ministerial mission of salvation in history: the apostolic college. And there is only one divine ministerial mission: that which Christ entrusted to the apostolic college and which is handed on to its successor, the college of bishops.

[2] Cf. Vatican Council I, Constitution *Pastor Aeternus* (Denz. 1821-3050); Vatican Council II, *Constitution on the Church,* n. 18, which refers back to Vatican Council I.

II
FROM DIVINE MISSION TO CANONICAL MISSION

The divine mission entrusted to the college is universal: in time—"till the consummation of the world"; in space—"to the whole world"; in relation to people—"to all the nations"; in its ministry—"whatever you shall loose. . . ." and "as the Father has sent me with all power, so also I send you. . . ." It is the task of the apostolic college to organize itself so as to be capable of carrying out its historical mission historically in history. To do this it has to embrace new members so as to prolong itself in time (apostolic succession) and to spread throughout the whole world and among all men (by establishing local Churches new in locale and in men): one member will be an apostle to the Jews, another to the Gentiles, and each will take care not to interfere where another is already preaching (cf. Rom. 15, 16-20; Gal. 2, 7-8).

Thus the college, through requirements inseparable from its historical fulfilling of its universal historical mission, is bound to set up a canonical ordering, a missionary-pastoral organization and a plan of action.

The college incorporates new members through a specific act, called the sacrament of orders, which has from the outset been carried out by the laying on of hands. By his incorporation, each new member is made a participator, a sharer, a *sponsor,* or rather a *communicator* in the universal collegial mission, and so in the function (*munus*), in the duty (*officium*) and in the task (*cura*) of the mission, and in the functions, ministries, authority and spiritual powers of the college, which are implicit in the collegial mission shared through communion.

When each new member communicates or receives in this way, he communicates personally (*personaliter: Constitution on the Church,* n. 27), and so he personally is a "missionary", an emissary or vicar of Christ, but he communicates, becomes and is this through being and insofar as he is a member of the college—through communion in the college. He must therefore act as a member of a college which has a head and other collegiate members—that is, within the hierarchical communion, within the ordering or missionary-pastoral organization and program which define the college (cf. *Constitution on the Church,* n. 21; *Decree on the Ministry and Life of Priests,* n. 7).

Through this canonical programming the college binds the task of each member into the joint task of the collegial program of action, giving to each member the task of carrying out his functions and exercising his powers, both of which he receives by communion in the college, in particular circumstances or ways, and so the college sends each member out in a communion of office. This particularized assignation of tasks and this definite historical sending-out constitute what is called the canonical mission.

III

THE AUTHORITY OF THE COLLEGE
OVER THE CANONICAL MISSION

The college, by formulating its program, automatically renders any action contrary to it illegitimate. This is not an indication of any desire to impose new obligations, but a reflection of the need to make the functioning of the hierarchical communion clear in particular circumstances, to realize the duty of historical order and efficacy and to avoid confusion and ineffectiveness. Even more: this need for order in missionary activity is so pressing that the college even renders actions contrary to its program of action *null*—for instance, the nullity of confession or witness to a marriage that has taken place without the due "ministerial licenses".[3]

Furthermore, just as the college divided and distributed time

[3] Taking the canonically established *de facto* capacities, twelve main grades or categories of members of the college can be distinguished. Cf. my article on the power of the Church over the faculty of orders and over the sacraments in the light of canonical logic, in *Rev. Esp. Teol.* 22 (1962).

(apostolic succession) and space and people (local Churches), so historically it had to divide and distribute the different ministries implied in the universal divine mission. In order to historically guarantee the efficacy of execution of the missionary task, it has come to refuse to incorporate or confer a higher grade of communion in its mission than that required by the exercise of the particular missionary venture demanded by the program. It does not fully incorporate or give full communion in the mission and its effects to those it enrolls as "collaborators", but shares and distributes different grades of the sacrament of orders. And so members come to have different ranks within the college; in effect, the college has created a "presbyteral order" next to the "episcopal order" as its help and organ, and a "diaconal order" to serve them both.

IV

THE NATURE AND HISTORICAL FORMS
OF THE CANONICAL MISSION

Such, then, is the historical nature of the universal divine mission. An evaluation of it in itself and in the various historical embodiments of its program leads to attributing to the college the power of organizing itself and structuring itself according to the requirements of its mission in each age or according to the "signs of the times".[4] This leads, once again, to the thesis of the generic foundation by Christ of the college and its operation.

Theologically—that is, through the nature of the divine mission and its implications and by the mandatory nature of revelation—the college can decide its organization or concrete structure canonically as suits it best for the fulfillment of its mission. It can do this either by dividing its sacrament into grades and estab-

---

[4] Vatican Council II, *Constitution on the Church in the Modern World*, n. 44: "Since the Church has a visible and social structure . . . she can and ought to be enriched by the development of human social life. The reason is not that the constitution given her by Christ is defective, but . . . [to] adjust it more successfully to our times."

lishing in its midst the categories or orders it requires, or it can make laws governing merely the functioning of these grades, conditioning the licitness alone, or also the validity, of the ministerial task.

History confirms this outline view. In the past, the normal structure has been the pyramidal one, with particular individuals occupying different ranks in the hierarchical structure: the Roman pontiff, responsible for the universal Church and tracing his origins back to divine institution; then the patriarch, primate, metropolitan or archbishop; then, in descending rank, bishop, coadjutor bishop, dean or archpriest, parish priest. But past and present also show the structure of hierarchical levels of colleges or collegial government: ecumenical council, international plenary, national plenary, provincial plenary, and the collegiate government of several bishops in one diocese (as seems to have generally occurred up to the middle of the 3rd century). And today we find the rather more sophisticated form of international, national and provincial bishops' conferences.[5] At other times, the personal and collegial forms have combined, with the leaders of each lower circle forming the higher circle. Until the eve of Vatican Council II, metropolitan conferences functioned in this way, and since the Council, the synod of bishops has taken on much the same form. Thus the canonical mission affects the role of each individual member as well as that of the collegiate organs themselves.[6]

The same is true of presbyters and deacons and their distribu-

[5] The difference between episcopal conferences and councils is not a theological one, but only of ritual solemnity and particular canonical function and capacity. Cf. *Decree on the Pastoral Office of Bishops in the Church*, n. 38. The fifth Lateran Council said: "After the ascension the apostles distributed bishops to each city and diocese, as the Holy Roman Church set them up throughout the world, distributing by degrees the office of patriarch, primate, archbishop and bishop; and it was also laid down by the sacred canons that . . . in order to carry out the commands of the Lord there should be held provincial councils and episcopal synods."

[6] Vatican Council II makes this clear by saying that the college cannot exercise its full and complete power "without the consent of the Roman pontiff"; it is a fact that the head of the college must call it to legal

tion. Formerly, with the doctrine of collegiality in the doldrums, missionary organization was reserved to the exclusive competence of the Holy See (Canon 1350), and each bishop only ordained those priests he needed for his local Church (cf. Canon 969). But the bishops can now make a more efficient distribution of those who form their "organ and help"—that is, the order of presbyters and the order of deacons, as is stated in the Council's *Decree on the Ministry and Life of Priests* (n. 10).

Each bishop is incardinated as a full member (*co-optatus*) of the episcopal order, and each presbyter or deacon as a cooperator (*co-aptatus*) with the episcopal order" (*Constitution on the Church,* n. 28), and by virtue of this he is in the service of the universal divine mission in which he communicates, in the service of the universal Church. This theological incardination leads through the canonical mission to direct canonical incardination in a local Church, but it could also lead to incardination directly into episcopal conferences or patriarchates, from which distribution would be made to the local Churches as needs dictated, or to different jobs. The Council's *Decree on the Church's Missionary Activity* (cf. n. 20) appears to point in this direction.

V
CONCLUSION

The permanent concern of the college is a form of canonical mission that will be effective at each moment in history. It is important in this context to realize that the episcopal order does not have its hands tied too tightly by the theological bases. It is vital that the historical fact of the canonical mission, as it has functioned so far, should be considered not as something that can neither be touched nor changed, but as something gifted with the full possibilities of the universal divine mission.

---

action, or at least "freely accept" it. Cf. *Constitution on the Church,* n. 22; cf. also the prefatory note of explanation.

To the extent that the college fails to formulate its canonical mission correctly, and fails to carry it out through each and every one of its members, it fails in efficacy in applying its divine mission to the historical context. The canonical mission is not a sort of ad-libbed superstructure, but a historical necessity derived from the historical character of the universal divine mission. And the necessity becomes all the greater as history progressively complicates the execution of the divine mission and as the college keeps growing, thereby causing the growth of the Church which it convokes and forms.

The canonical mission does not actually *give* anything; it does not add anything to the rights received by ordination and incorporation into the college, nor does it validate these rights, as if ordination gave only a sort of "ontological-sacramental" faculty or participation, incomplete in itself and requiring completion by the addition of something extra. No, the canonical mission is limited in its effects to regulating the historical activities of the members of the college and to defining the living forms of the hierarchical communion.

The canonical mission shows the free and expedient canonical way of exercising the powers conferred on each member by ordination and incorporation into the college. It declares the exercise of functions in conformity with its ordering to be legitimate, and those exercised outside the lines of the canonical program to be illegitimate (invalid or illicit). It is an authorization to exercise the authority and powers conferred by the sacrament, an authorization that the college must formulate in an endless variety of ways according to the "signs of the times" to which it is applying the universal divine mission.[7]

[7] The foregoing can also be applied, except in differing degrees, to the divine mission, in which all Christians participate as members of the body of Christ (cf. *Decree on the Church's Missionary Activity,* n. 5), and through the canonical missions they receive (cf. *Decree on the Apostolate of the Laity,* n. 24).

Eugenio Corecco/*Munich, West Germany*

The Bishop as Head of the Local Church and Its Discipline

I

THE CHURCH, SACRAMENT OF THE TRINITY

The Church, like every Christian mystery, has her origin in the mystery of the unity and plurality of the Trinity, and it is in the Trinity that she has her ultimate explanation.[1] Therefore, it is impossible to explain the Church in terms merely of philosophy or history,[2] for there is a tension in the Church which derives from the fact of many local Churches existing within the one universal Church, and this tension remains insoluble without a religious explanation, since the Church "is the people brought together in the union of the Father, Son and Holy Spirit".[3] This polyvalent nature of the Church has been taken into account from the very beginning of theological reflection. St. Paul, followed by St. Cyprian, gave to the term "church" both a local and a universal meaning.[4] In patristic thought the universal view of

[1] M. Philipon, "La santissima Trinità et la Chiesa," in *La Chiesa del Vaticano II* (Florence, 1965), pp. 328-31; E. Zoghby, "Unità e diversità della Chiesa," *ibid.*, pp. 525, 535-37.
[2] W. Beinert, "Die Una Catholica und die Partikularkirche," in *Theol. u. Phil.* 42 (1967), pp. 3-5.
[3] Vat. Eccl. 4, 2 (Documenti, Il Concilio Vaticano, ed. Dehoniane).
[4] Cf. K. Rahner, *Episkopat und Primat* (Quaest. Disputatae 11) (Freiburg im Br., 1961), pp. 21-30; G. Dejaifve, "La collegialità nella tradizione latina," in *La Chiesa del Vaticano II, op. cit.*, pp. 838-40; J. Hajjar, "La collegialità nella tradizione orientale," *ibid.*, pp. 816-17.

the Church seems to have dominated,[5] while in the living structure of the Church there prevailed in early times the local Church, which was directly experienced in practical Christian life. In both East and West, theology and practice developed independently of each other, with little reference from one to the other, and this gave rise to differing ecclesiologies and systems of Canon Law, which were to be the fundamental cause in their turn for the final break which came at the great schism.[6]

II
The Theology of the Local Church: Communion

The Idea of the Church

The ecclesiology embodied in the idea of communion, although found elsewhere, is typical of Eastern theology. It approaches the problem of the Church empirically; starting with the datum of the local community, Eastern theology attributes to it a content based on a history and anthropology quite different from the Western view. While Latin theology emphasized rather the characteristics of the Church as in this world, Eastern theology showed an Hellenistic taste for the characteristics of the spiritual side of the Church. The Church is like an icon; she is the sacrament of the heavenly, spiritual, realities. Such an ecclesiology is essentially sacramental and eucharistic, based on the local community, which is always seen as a constant, perfect manifes-

---

[5] A. Schmemann, "La notion de primauté dans l'ecclésiologie orthodoxe," in *La primauté de Pierre dans l'Eglise Orthodoxe* (Neuchâtel, 1960), p. 141; M.-J. Le Guillou, "L'expérience orientale de la collégialité éiscopale et ses requêtes," in *La collégialité épiscopale* (Unam Sanctam 52) (Paris, 1965), p. 176; Y. Congar, "De la communion des Eglises à une ecclésiologie de l'Eglise universelle," in *L'Episcopat de l'Eglise Universelle* (Unam Sanctam 39) (Paris, 1962), p. 228.

[6] On this whole question, and in particular on sections II and III of this article, cf. Y. Congar, *Neuf cent ans aprees. Notes sur le "Schisme oriental"* (Irénikon) (Chevetogne, 1954), pp. 16-181; idem, "De la communion. . . ," *loc. cit.*, pp. 227-60; idem, "Notes sur le destin de l'idée de collégialité épiscopale en Occident au Moyen Age (VII—XVI siècles)," in *La collégialité épiscopale, op. cit.*, pp. 99-129.

tation of the universal Church. The basic principle governing the relations between local Churches was the concept of realizing in a concrete way the universal alliance in Christ that obtains between the various churches in the οἰκουμενη. This was achieved not merely by norms dictated from above, but rather by the various practices developed by the Churches themselves, whether at the personal level—letters, hospitality and service—or in their liturgical contacts (εὐλογια, the *fermentum* and excommunication), or in the later development of institutional contacts (synods and synodal letters).[7] The role of the bishop of Rome in this inter-Church activity was merely relative. He was considered not so much as an authority with power derived from a divine right higher than the other bishops, but more as the custodian of the Church's unity, with power not *over* the Church but rather *within* the ecclesial communion.[8] And this communion in its turn depended rather on a bond of love in the Holy Spirit (*sobornost*) than on the legal position of a monarchical authority deriving from the possession of an ecclesiastical office.[9]

Synods

This ecclesiology was interpreted by the orthodox in terms of an acephalous synodal system.[10] Since the Church ought faithfully to reflect the equality which obtains between the persons of

[7] Cf. Y. Congar, "De la communion. . . ," *loc. cit.*, pp. 231-35.

[8] Cf. A. Alivisatos, "Les conciles oecuméniques, V, VI, VII, VIII," in *Le Concile et les Conciles* (Unam Sanctam) (Chevetogne, 1960), p. 120; H. Marot, "Conciles anténicéens et conciles oecuméniques," *ibid.*, pp. 42-43.

[9] M.-J. Le Guillou, *Mission et Unité. Les exigeances de la communion* (Unam Sanctam 34) (Paris, 1960), pp. 184-200; E. Ivanea, "Sobornost," in *Lex Theol. und Kirche* 9 (Freiburg,[2] 1964), pp. 841-42.

[10] This acephalous arrangement is not necessarily restricted to the synodal regime only. It is also possible within a monarchical system; cf. the medieval Byzantine theologians on the doctrine of "pentarchy"; cf. V. Pospischil, *Der Patriarch in der Serbisch-Orthodoxen Kirche* (Wien, 1966), pp. 63-78. See also *Loi organique de l'Eglise autocéphale de Grèce* (1923) and *Charte constitutionelle de l'Eglise de Grèce*, published in *Istina* 7 (1960), pp. 153-72, 279-300, where it is clear that the Holy Synod is the supreme legislative, administrative and judicial organ of the autocephalous Church of Greece.

the Trinity, and since also the bishops, by reason of their consecration, are equal among themselves, the structure of the
synods was of equals among equals; the ultimate level of authority was never any particular individual, but the body of bishops as a whole.[11] The institution which best reflects this ecclesiology is the synod *endemousa,* by virtue of which the Byzantine
Church considers itself as being permanently gathered in synod.
In this situation, the position of the patriarch is quite different
from that of the pope. The pope governed the Roman synod and
also claimed authority over the ecumenical synod, in addition to
the power he obtained in later times over the provincial councils.
But in the Byzantine Church the synod cannot proceed without
the patriarch, nor can he make final decisions without reference
to the synod.[12]

The Function of the Bishop

The image of the bishop as a mystical and cultic figure takes
precedence over the canonical and juridical idea of his function.
The bishop is seen as the type of the Father in the life of the
Church; he is the liturgical figure who unites the whole of the
local community in a twofold movement: their return to the Father and their bond of communion with all the other Churches.[13]
The collegial aspect of the bishop's function was seen as being so
important[14] that any higher personal authority of a monarchical
nature was quite excluded. The authority of the bishops at the
local level was all the stronger for this. The higher bishops (patriarchs and metropolitans) have their various powers only insofar as these are acknowledged as theirs by the whole body of

[11] M.-J. Le Guillou, *Mission et Unité* II, *op. cit.,* p. 189.
[12] J. Hajjar, "La collegialità nella tradizione orientale," in *La chiesa
del Vaticano II, op. cit.,* pp. 818-31; *idem,* "Synode permanent et collégialité épiscopale dans l'Eglise byzantine au premier millénaire," in
La collégialité épiscopale, op. cit., pp. 151-66.
[13] Th. Strotmann, "L'evêque dans la tradition orientale," in *l'Episcopat
et l'Eglise Universelle, op. cit.,* pp. 309-314. Latin theology usually prefers
to compare the bishop to Christ; cf. J. Pascher, "Die Hierarchie in
sakramentaler Symbolik," in *Studien über das Bischofsamt* (Regensburg,
1949), p. 292.
[14] J. Hajjar, "La collegialità. . . ," *op. cit.,* p. 823.

bishops (ecumenical councils and the patriarchal synod).[15] When translated into juridical terms, this became a system of concessions. However, these were not concessions granted from above, as in the Latin Church, but rather from below, a system which thus eliminated the possibility of any personal interference within the sphere of jurisdiction which belonged to the lower bishop. Thus at the local level, the bishop enjoyed considerable autonomy of action.[16]

III

THE THEOLOGY OF THE UNIVERSAL CHURCH

The Concept of the Church

Because of the West's different eucharistic theology, Latin ecclesiology developed along its own lines. In the East, the idea of transcendence was much to the fore, and in the breaking of bread the bishops are seen as all representing Christ in the same way. In the West, however, there was a more juridical view of the eucharist, seeing it rather as a sacrifice of reconciliation, in keeping with the power of binding and loosing. The redemptive act, which is celebrated by the bishops in the eucharistic sacrifice, is performed in a special way by the successor of Peter (Mt. 16, 19), who therefore enjoys primacy over all the others.[17] The Augustinian view of the eucharist was that the local celebration is a reflection of the unity of the local Church; this idea was taken up in a one-sided way by the Middle Ages. "Church" became synonymous with the whole body, incorporating all believ-

[15] V. Pospischil, *op. cit.*, pp. 64-65. For the discusion over the existence of absolute rights belonging to the person of the patriarch, see especially pp. 69-72.

[16] Cf. the list of the rights of the patriarchs and metropolitans in N. Milasch, *Das Kirchenrecht der morgenländischen Kirche* (Mostar,[2] 1905), pp. 326-29, 335-38. On the rights of bishops in an "eparchy" (diocese), cf. *ibid.*, pp. 372-86, 456-58.

[17] C. Andresen, "Geschichte der abendländischen Konzile des Mittelalters," in *Die ökumenischen Konzile der Christenheit* (Stuttgart, 1961), pp. 79-84.

ers in a vertical structure.[18] The "Church of Rome", understood at one time as referring to the local Church, became equivalent to the "Catholic Church", reflecting a kind of imperial, universal vision. The decretals, typical of the Latin mentality, incorporated this vision into a system of discipline, tending to reduce all to uniformity. With the Gregorian reform in the West, the Church detached herself from the feudal theocratic structure, and this enabled her to define herself as a perfect society, with her own autonomy and law, as distinct from the secular power [19] and to transform herself into some sort of vast diocese, into which even the new religious orders were directly incorporated.[20] The pope has the *plenitudo potestatis;* he is the *fons et origo* of all ecclesial life and the first bishop of every diocese.[21] The principle underlying his relations with the bishops appears now as the appointment of each pastor *in partem sollicitudinis papae;* consequently, Catholic doctrine reduces the bishop to the position of a mere vicar or legate of the pope.[22]

Synods

This all-embracing pyramid scheme of the Latin Church implies also a different view of councils. General councils appear in

[18] B. Neunheuser, "Chiesa universale et chiesa locale," in *La chiesa del Vaticano II, op. cit.,* pp. 628-30.

[19] Y. Congar, "L'ecclesiologie de la Révolution française au Concile du Vatican, sous le signe de l'affirmation de l'autorité," in *L'ecclésiologie au XIXᵉ siècle* (Unam Sanctam 34) (Paris, 1960), p. 90.

[20] O. Rousseau, "La doctrine du ministère épiscopale et ses vicissitudes dans l'Eglise d'Occident," in *L'Episcopat et l'Eglise Universelle, op. cit.,* pp. 286-87.

[21] The quarrel between the seculars and mendicants in the 13th century, which was more than a mere controversy over spirituality, had an influence on ecclesiology; cf. J. Ratzinger, "Der Einfluss des Bettelordens-streites auf die Entwicklung der Lehre vom päpstlichen universalprimat, unter besondered Berüchsichtigung des heiligen Bonaventura," in *Theol. in der Geschlichte un Gegenwart* (Munich, 1957), pp. 697-724; Y. Congar, "Aspects ecclésiologiques de la querelle entre mendiants et séculiers dans la seconde moitié du XIIIᵉ et le début du XIVᵉ siècles," in *Arch. Hist. Doctr. Lit.* (1961), pp. 35-151.

[22] Y. Congar, "De la communion. . . ," *loc. cit.,* pp. 238f.; cf. also J. Rivière, "In partem sollicitudinis . . . Evolution d'une formule pontificale," in *Rev. Sc. Relig.* 5 (1925), pp. 210-31.

the West not so much as assemblies of bishops meeting together;
rather, they appear as representatives from all Christianity to
offer advice to the supreme pontiff. The pope is the head, the
bishops the members. They are not present on an equal footing,
nor even as a body, but as individuals.[23] With the Council of
Trent, the episcopate recovered *de facto* its collegial responsibilities.[24] However, ecclesiology, under pressure from Protestant-
ism and Gallicanism, became yet more centered on the papacy
and the universal Church, thus overshadowing the concept of
communion in favor of the "society" aspect as contained in the
idea of juridical primacy.[25] This increasingly undermined the
autonomy and strength of the particular councils of the local
Churches.[26]

The Function of the Bishop [27]

As a result of the tension in the relations between the local
and universal Church, the juridical idea of the bishop has fluctu-
ated considerably in the West. As in the East until the 14th
century, the authority of the bishop as head of the local Church

[23] C. Andresen, *loc. cit.*, pp. 75-149; G. Fransen, "L'ecclésiologie des
conciles médiévaux," in *Le Concile et les Conciles, op. cit.*, pp. 125-41;
H. Jedin, *Struktur-probleme der ökumenischen Konzilien* (Cologne,
1963), pp. 2-27.

[24] The conciliarism in the Council of Constance had little true feeling
for collegiality, in spite of its insisting on an "ecclesiology of the Church";
cf. C. Moeller, "La collégialité au Concile de Constance," in *La collégialité épiscopale, op. cit.*, p. 149.

[25] On the ecclesiology of the period, cf. Y. Congar, "Kirche. II Dog-
mengeschichtelich," in *Handbuch Theologischer Grundbegriffe* I (Munich,
1962), pp. 807-12; cf. also H. Fries, III Systematisch, *ibid.*, pp. 812-22.

[26] From the time of Trent until the end of the 19th century, approximately 260 provincial or plenary councils were held in the Latin Church.
If we take 90 as the minimum number of ecclesiastical provinces, it
looks as if the number of councils during this time was approximately
2% of the number laid down by Church law. Cf. E. Corecco, *La forma-
zione della Chiesa negli Stati Uniti d'America attraverso l'attività sino-
dale, con particolare riguardo al problem dell' amministrazione dei beni
ecclesiastici* (Munich, 1962).

[27] For this whole question, cf. W. Plöchl, *Geschichte des Kirchenrechts*
I (Vienna,[2] 1960), pp. 342-33, 165-66; II ([2]1962), pp. 141-44; III
(1959), pp. 257-58; H. Feine, *Kirchliche Rechtsgeschichte* (Cologne,
[4]1964), pp. 124-27, 213-19, 364-79, 533-39.

is unquestioned *(ein gewaltiger Herr)*.[28] His position is based
on the possession of a legitimate function, and his judical and
administrative authority is expressed symbolically in the one
eucharist which is shared by the whole presbyterate and people.[29] His decisions are taken in the light of the advice given by
the presbyterate, the wishes of the people and local tradition.
When the Church found herself obliged to adapt to the pressure
of the politico-religious unity of a new world, the bishop was
changed into the local administrator, representing an omni-
present civil and ecclesiastical government, a development which
effectively depersonalized his relations with the local community
(cf. the practice of absolute ordination). Progressive centralization by Rome certainly weakened the position of metropolitans
(now considered merely as an extension of the papal primacy);
it also reduced the status of bishops in the West, who had indeed
consolidated their position by establishing both their private (cf.
the system of the "proper Church) and public rights (feudal
functions, *bannus*). But now they resembled more the suffragan
bishops who held the suburban sees.[30]

Episcopal authority was also threatened in the internal government of the diocese; from the early Middle Ages the spread of
the parochial structure had gradually broken up the presbyterate,
transforming the priest into a minister who enjoyed his own
proper rights and had lost for the most part any collegial link
with his bishop.[31] The late Middle Ages saw the granting of
innumerable privileges and exemptions (convents, religious orders, foundations and universities). This, plus the policy of bene-

[28] U. Stutz, *Kirchenrecht* (Sonderabzug, 1904), pp. 825-26.

[29] In Milan and Carthage at the end of the 4th century, there was
only one eucharist for the whole city on Sundays; cf. V. Monachino,
La cura pastorale a Milano, Cartagine e Roma nel secolo IV (Rome,
1947), pp. 55-56, 188-90.

[30] For the three different areas in which the influence of Rome was
felt, cf. P. Batiffol, *Cathedra Petri* (Unam Sanctam 4) (Paris, 1938),
pp. 41-59.

[31] B. Bazatole, "L'evêque et la vie chrétienne au sein de l'Eglise locale,"
in *L'Episcopat et L'Eglise Universelle, op. cit.*, pp. 342-48. For the
history of the development of the parish, cf. A. Blöchlinger, *Die heutige
Pfarrei als Gemeinschaft* (Einsiedeln, 1962), pp. 57-122.

fices adopted by the Holy See (reservations), backed by the particular law and *consuetudo*, served to exaggerate the position of cathedral chapters, the higher prelates (archdeacons and auxiliary bishops) and the laity (right of patronage).

This twofold weakening of the bishop in his relations both with those below and above him was embodied likewise in Scholastic theology. The power of jurisdiction, now seen as independent of the power of orders,[32] was taken as a mere extension of the papal power of orders, while as far as the power of orders was concerned the bishop was not really distinguished from the *simplex sacerdos* (the same power of order, the non-sacramental nature of the episcopate).[33] The medieval universalist culture was able to conceive authority only in the form of a leader in command of a body; thus the bishop was viewed in isolation, a papal representative linked to a locality,[34] bound by an oath of obedience and obliged to an *ad limina* visit. He was underrated, both as guardian of the local Church, because of interference by third parties, and as a link with other Churches and the universal Church, since in spite of intense synodal activity, the Middle Ages had little idea of what episcopal collegiality really was.[35]

The Tridentine reform did understand to an extent that the ecclesial crisis originated in this imbalance which had weakened the episcopal office. Unable to resolve the basic question of the human or divine origin of the bishop's jurisdiction, the Council

[32] On this question, cf. K. Mörsdorf, "Die Entwicklung der Zweigliedrigkeit der kirchlichen Hierarchie," in *Münchener Theol. Zeit.* 3 (1952), pp. 1-16; K. Nasilowski, *De distinctione potestatis in ordine in primaeva canonistarum doctrina* (Munich, 1962); E. Corecco, "L'origine del potere di giurisdizione episcopale: aspetti storico-giuridici e metodologico-sistematici della questione," in *La Scuola Cattolica* 96 (1968).

[33] O. Rousseau, *loc. cit.*, pp. 279-96.

[34] Y. Congar, "Notes sur le destin," *loc. cit.*, pp. 113-27; G. Alberigo, *Lo sviluppo della dottrina sui poteri nella Chiesa universale* (Rome, 1964), pp. 4-7.

[35] According to Y. Congar (*ibid.*, pp. 118-27), the idea of episcopal collegiality was "abolished" in the Middle Ages by the doctrine of the divine right of the college of cardinals. Cf. also M. Garcia Miralles, "El Cardinalato de institutione divina y el Episcopado en el problema de la succesiòn apostòlica según Juan de Torquemada," in *XVI Semana Española de Teologia* (Madrid, 1957), pp. 249-74.

tried instead to cope with the difficult problem of how to strengthen not only the papal power but also the power of the bishops.[36] This it did by the pragmatic device of *delegatio a jure,* which conferred on bishops—"loaned" to them, as it were—faculties which were considered proper to the position of the pope.[37] To counteract the abuses arising from the innumerable exemptions, the Council restored the right of the ordinary to visit and to supervise (especially with reference to the administration of ecclesiastical property), and recognized his right to legislate in his own territory without papal approval, and to dispense in particular cases from the common law. Obligations were also laid down for the bishop (residence) helping thus to reestablish a higher image.[38] This was not yet a true restoration of the powers of the bishop, because once again he was considered, as also in the Code of 1917, as being too dependent on the papacy. The whole ecclesiological structure still overemphasized the individual and did not sufficiently take into account the bishop's function and his collegial responsibility.

IV

THE REFORM OF VATICAN COUNCIL II

The Council's Ecclesiology

The particular value of the local Church was stated in Vatican Council II, as it had been in no other council.[39] However, taken overall in the teaching of the Council, the local Church is still

---

[36] W. Bertrams, "De quaestione circa originem potestatis iurisdictionis episcoporum in concilio tridentino non resoluta," in *Periodica Rer. Mor. Can. Lit.* 52 (1963), pp. 458-62; G. Alberigo, *op. cit.,* pp. 11-101; H. Grisar, "Die Frage des päpstlichen Primates und des Ursprunges der bischöflichen Gewalten auf dem Tridentinum," in *Zeitschr. f. kath. Theol.* 8 (1884), pp. 453-507, 727-84.

[37] E. Rösser, *Die gesetzliche Delegation* (Paderborn, 1937), pp. 113-27.

[38] H. Jedin, *Das Bischofsideal der katholischen Reformation* (Bruges, 1953).

[39] F. Kantzenbach, "Luthers Konzilstheologoie und die Gegenwart," in *Luth. Monatshefte* 5 (1966), p. 169.

seen in a slightly impersonal way, as the situation by means of which the universal Church is made manifest.[40] The fundamental principle relating to the local Church was introduced very late in the history of the schema of the *Constitution on the Church*, so that it did not exercise the same overall influence as the idea of the universal Church. However, the fact remains that the Council provided full justification for an ecclesiology which centers on the eucharistic community.[41] The temptation was overcome to take the local Church merely as an administrative unit of the universal Church, and in fact its existence is based on dogmatic reasons, and not only on historico-sociological ones. The particular Church does realize in itself the universal Church, insofar as in the bishop's celebration of Word and sacrament there is made present the mystery of the Trinity; it offers at the same time the essential meeting point for men to come into contact with the mystery of salvation,[42] a mystery which indeed is fully represented in the symbol of the universal Church,[43] which is, in Christ, the sacrament of the union both with God and with the whole human race.[44]

Now the unity of the Church is derived not from uniformity but from her plurality,[45] and the local Churches, in their own, proper way, are an essential part in an ascending hierarchy to be found fully explained in the Council (patriarchate, diocese, parish, house church[46] and separated ecclesial communities[47]). The Council did not take up any position with regard to the debated question whether the universal Church was prior to the local Church or vice versa. In fact there exists both the structure

---

[40] Cf. W. Beinert, *loc. cit.*, pp. 8-9.

[41] K. Rahner, "Das Zweite Vatikanische Konzil, Kommentare I," in *Lex. Theol. und Kirche* (Freiburg, 1966), pp. 242-45.

[42] W. Beinert, *loc. cit.*, pp. 10-11.

[43] The local Church is the symbol of the whole ecclesial body only by virtue of its communion with the universal Church. Ecclesial communion is a dimension which transcends the merely local Church.

[44] Vat. Eccl. 1.

[45] Vat. Eccl. 13.

[46] Vat. Eccl. 11, 2; Vat. Laic. 11, 4.

[47] Vat. Oec. 13.

belonging to the universal Church (primacy and episcopal college) and the structure characteristic of the local Church (the episcopal office).[48] Christ did not give priority in his institution either to the local Church or to the universal Church;[49] rather, he founded the Church as such, with her own twofold structure, whose parts are complementary.

The Collegial Structure

Beginning with her own concrete experience, the early Church always considered the idea of the college of bishops as secondary to the concept of the local Church. Modern theology has never experienced directly the Church as active in her councils; theology is under the influence of illuminism even yet. Hence the theological approach to this problem has been speculative rather than historical.[50] And so, the Latin theology of the universal Church influenced Vatican Council II more with reference to the Church's structure—collegiality—than at the purely ecclesiological level. In fact the Council did not recognize the true character of collegiality in the strict sense, and rather took as its central points the problem of the relations of the bishop to the papal primacy and the question whether the subject of power was single or twofold.[51]

If the Council did reappraise the shape and form of local councils,[52] with particular reference to the modern form of the episcopal conference,[53] it nevertheless did not apply the idea of

[48] Y. Congar, "Neuf cent ans après," op. cit., pp. 84-85.

[49] This point of view was put forward by Archbishop Veuillot in his relatio on the Textus Emendatus, 1964; cf. K. Mörsdorf, "Kommentare II," op. cit., p. 151, n. 4.

[50] J. Ratzinger, "La collegialità episcopale: spiegzione teologica," in La Chiesa del Vaticano II, op. cit., pp. 745-47.

[51] On this point, cf. W. Bertrams, Il potere pastorale del papa e del collegio dei vescovi (Rome, 1967), pp. 62-122; C. Colombo, "Costituzione gerarchica della Chiesa e in particolare dell'episcopato," in La Costituzione "De Ecclesia" (Milan, 1965), pp. 237-61; K. Mörsdorf, "Primat und Kollegialität nach dem Konzil," in Uber das bischöfliche Amt (Karlsruhe, 1966), pp. 42-45.

[52] Vat. Ep. 36.

[53] Vat. Ep. 37-38; Eccl. Sanc. I, 41.

collegiality to them, putting aside the hypothesis that they could be a way of sharing in the supreme power of the universal college.[54] In fact, they are a genuine form of collegiality, of a local kind, and differ from universal collegiality in that they do not enjoy power over the whole Church. While the Code of Canon Law had seen in the episcopal conference only an institution which derived from the papal primacy, Vatican Council II recognized the local collegial gathering as an institution whose ultimate justification was the proper, ordinary power of the bishops. In particular, it made the episcopal conference a real intermediary between the central authority and the local bishop, in a position now to exercise a more general form of authority, and not only in particular cases.[55]

The Function of the Bishop

1. *The Local Church as the Criterion of the Bishop's Function.* The bishop, from both the theological and juridical point of view, emerged from Vatican Council II with his position radically revised, in his relationship both with higher authority and with the local Church. The doctrine of collegiality has underlined his juridical and moral responsibility to the whole Church. The reconsideration of the position of the local Church has restored the original responsibility of the bishop for the local Church. Now the local Church is an ecclesial body only insofar as it is able to show forth the essential characteristics of the universal Church, and likewise the bishop is only the local Church's legitimate head, insofar as he is a member of the college of bishops. Therefore, the local Church should be taken as the criterion by which the function of the bishop may be defined, since he presides over the local Church and is its representative in the assembly of bishops.[56] Thus we can see that it was not

[54] A distinction should be made between formal and material collegiality. Cf. W. Aymans, *Das synodale Element in der Kirchenverfassung* (Munich, 1967), Chapter 4, Part I.

[55] On this whole problem, cf. K. Mörsdorf, *Kommentare II, op. cit.,* pp. 228-32, 237-38.

[56] K. Rahner, "Bischof und Bistum," in *Handbuch der Pastoraltheologie* I (Freiburg, 1964), pp. 167-79.

only for reasons of administration that Vatican Council II, for the first time in the history of the councils, was concerned with the definition of the nature of a diocese.[57]

2. *The Personal Aspect of the Bishop's Power.* Analogously to the universal Church, there is within the diocese a personal principle of unity and a collegial principle.[58] The bishop is the personal principle, insofar as he possesses by divine right the complete power of orders and jurisdiction necessary to carry out his apostolic duties of teaching, sanctifying and ruling.[59] The Council completely reversed the whole approach to the episcopal office by fully restoring the bishop to the position he originally enjoyed—and still enjoys to an extent in the Oriental tradition.

The power of orders of the bishop was not defined by the Council by referring it to the priestly power of orders, but rather the other way around, and the sacramental fullness of the priesthood was predicated of the bishop.[60] With reference to the power of jurisdiction, on the other hand, the Council eliminated any possibility of seeing such jurisdiction as deriving from the papal primacy by affirming explicitly that the individual bishop has, *per se* and in his own right, all the ordinary powers necessary for his apostolic function.[61]

From the system of the concession of powers by the pope to the bishop, it had been a natural step to the system of questions reserved to the pope. Since the divine right does not exist in the abstract but can only be realized in the process of history by the

[57] Vat. Ep. 11, 1; 22-23.

[58] On the subordination of the one principle to the other, cf. K. Mörsdorf, "Uber die Zuordnung des Kollegialitätsprinzips zu dem Prinzip der Einheit von Haupt und Leib in der hierarchischen Struktur der Kirchenverfassung," in *Wahrheit und Verkündigung, M. Schmaus zum 70 Geburtstag* II (Munich, 1967), pp. 1435-45.

[59] Vat. Eccl. 25-27. *Lumen Gentium* expressly makes a distinction between the office and the power, to avoid any confusion between the doctrine on the triple office of the bishop and his "triple power". For the relationship between the power of orders and jurisdiction and the triple office, cf. K. Mörsdorf, "Heilige Gewalt," in *Sacramentum Mundi* II (Freiburg, 1967ff.).

[60] Vat. Eccl. 21, 2.

[61] Vat. Ep., 8/a.

development of human rights,[62] the problem is how to know in the concrete which powers are necessary for the bishop to be able to look after the discipline of his own local Church, so as to ensure that it is a valid manifestation of the universal Church. There is in fact a fundamental objection to the rigid juridical system of reservations. The office of bishop should indeed have limits laid down as to its content, lest the general legal presumption in favor of the bishop given by Vatican Council II degenerate into something completely arbitrary, but the problem obviously cannot be solved merely by the granting of a general faculty to dispense from the common law; [63] the bishop must also be able, in the revised Code of Canon Law, to influence directly, through his administrative and judicial activity, his own local discipline, taking into account the special characteristics and requirements of his own diocese.[64] Therefore, it is rather a question of restoring to the local Church its own internal autonomy and unity, which will make possible a pastoral policy for the diocese as a whole under the final responsibility of a single individual. This is the tendency, for example, of the norms of the Council which emphasize the global responsibility of the bishop in some sectors [65] and support this in a negative way by cancelling out the centrifugal tendency which took the clergy,[66] laity [67]

[62] K. Rahner, "Bischof und Bistum," loc. cit., p. 176; idem, "Uber den Begriff des 'Ius divinum' im kath. Verständnis," in Schriften zur Theologie V (Einsiedeln, 1962), pp. 249-77; idem, "Uber Bischofskonferenzen," ibid., VI (Einsiedeln, 1965), pp. 438-42.

[63] Vat. Ep. 8/b.

[64] On this whole question, cf. K. Mörsdorf, Kommentare II, op. cit., pp. 158-61, 166-71; idem, "Neue Vollmachten und Privilegien der Bischöfe," in Arch. f. kath. Kirchenrecht 133 (1964), pp. 82-101.

[65] While the Code of Canon Law attributed to the bishop a mainly negative function in supervising the execution of the liturgical norms (cf. Canon 1261), the Council abrogated Canon 1257 and returned to the bishop a general commission to supervise the liturgy in his diocese in keeping with the new law. Cf. Vat. Lit. 22, 1, Instr. Vat. Lit. 22; K. Mörsdorf, Lehrbuch des Kirchenrechts II (Paderborn, 11 1967, pp. 365-70.

[66] Vat. Ep. 31-32; Eccl. Sanc. 20-21. Cf. H. Schmitz, "Amtsenthebung und Versetzung der Pfarrer im neuen Recht," Trierer Theol. Zeitschr. 76 (1967), pp. 357-71.

[67] Vat. Ep. 28; Eccl. Sanc. I, 18.

and religious [68] away from the direct authority of the bishop. In a word, it is a question of translating into practical terms of law the picture of the bishop given in the *Decree on the Pastoral Office of Bishops in the Church*, nn. 11-16.[69]

3. *The Power of the Synod.* As pastoral activity develops in our industrial, consumer society which is seeing rapid expansion in every field, there is the risk of overtaxing the abilities of one individual. This consideration, and especially the fundamental theological teaching on the bishop, has led to a rediscovery of the further, lower, dimension of the episcopate. The bishop is rescued from the isolation into which he had fallen by several factors: the theological restoration of the presbyterate, the representation of priests in the shape of the council of priests,[70] and also, though only by analogy, the other councils and commissions on which religious [71] and also the laity have a consultative function. All of this is intended to involve every sector of the diocese and extend responsibility to the whole community. This isolation of the bishop was already known in the Middle Ages, when the idea of a unified pastoral policy was inconceivable, given the absence of any notion of collegiality [72]—a state of affairs which persisted even into recent times, in spite of a considerable missionary effort, under the guise of the partial exclusion of the bishop from the problems of the universal Church. The teaching on collegiality and on the local Church, which ought to reflect in the most authentic way possible the universal Church, was incorporated in the clear directives which came from the Council, with the purpose of preventing any kind of parochialism in the local Church, and rather promoting inter-

---

[68] Vat. Ep. 34-35; Eccl. Sanc. I, 22-40. A. Scheuermann, "Kommentar zum Ordensdekret des II Vatikanischen Konzils," in *Das Konzil und die Orden* (Cologne, 1967), pp. 105-08; *idem*, "Die Ausführungsbestimmungen zu den Konzilsweisungen für die Ordenzleute," *ibid.*, pp. 122-37.

[69] K. Mörsdorf, *Kommentare* II, *op. cit.*, p. 173.

[70] Cf. O. Saier, "Die hierarchische Struktur des Presbyteriums," in *Arch. f. kath. Kirchenrecht* 136 (1967), pp. 341-91; L. Weber, "Der Priesterrat," in *Der Seelsorger* 38 (1968), pp. 105-18.

[71] Religious are included among the diocesan clergy; cf. Vat. Ep. 34, 1.

[72] Y. Congar, "Notes sur le destin. . . ," *loc. cit.*, p. 118.

ecclesial responsibility—for example, a unified policy in pastoral theology,[73] in ecumenism [74] and in mission work.[75]

To sum up: the central teaching of the Council on episcopal collegiality has had the effect of restoring the standing of the bishop in the universal Church, while also strengthening his position as head of the local Church. Limits have been imposed on his authority—first from above, by incorporating him into an interdiocesan discipline, in the shape of an intermediate collegial institution (the episcopal conference), and second from below, by providing for the advisory function of the priests and laity.

[73] Cf., for example, Vat. Ep. 6; Vat. Presb. 10; Vat. Miss. 19, 4; 20, 1; Eccl. Sanc. I, 1-5.
[74] Cf., for example, Vat. Oec. 4, 11; 5; 10, 1.
[75] Cf., for example, Vat. Miss. 20; 38, 1-2.

Ferdinand Klostermann/*Vienna, Austria*

Supranational Episcopal Conferences

This article is concerned solely with supranational episcopal conferences. It does not concern itself with synods and councils, or even with episcopal organisms of the Church that are universal in scope. Its treatment is restricted to some of the problems relating specifically to this type of episcopal conference. Thus it also bypasses the problems faced by the Eastern rites, which favor the synodal approach and only use the looser format of an episcopal conference in urgent cases. Their use of the episcopal conference has been influenced by the Latin rite.

I
IMPORTANCE AND SCOPE

Canon 292, § 1 provides for episcopal conferences only on the provincial level, and they are without any sovereign authority; but other types of conferences could be subsumed under the introductory sentence. In fact, there were such things as supranational and continent-wide episcopal conferences long before Vatican Council II stipulated that "bishops of many nations can establish a single conference" (CD 38/5).[1] It was a necessary

[1] The following abbreviations are used in this article: (1) CD: Vatican

105

development, because a shrinking world called for a more wide-ranging interchange of study and planning within the Church. Without more organisms mediating between the Apostolic See and the various dioceses, Church decentralization would falter and the new revaluation of episcopal authority would degenerate into petty "diocesanism". Because of their unwieldiness, councils cannot take the place of episcopal conferences.

Essentially, the scope of supranational episcopal conferences embraces anything of international significance that relates to the welfare of souls. Conciliar and post-conciliar documents have expressly assigned certain tasks to episcopal conferences, and many of them could best be carried out by supranational episcopal conferences (see ES).

II

Their Legitimate Powers

In contrast to "contacts between episcopal conferences of different nations", which is highly recommended (CD 38/5), the establishment of supranational episcopal conferences is simply permitted "wherever special circumstances require it" (CD 38/5). "Of a given territory" (CD 38/1) refers to instances where the establishment of national conferences is impossible for some reason. But the "special circumstances" do not refer simply to that particular situation, even though a national episcopal conference is regarded as the normal thing. It does not exclude the possibility that supranational conferences will take on ever increasing importance, and that they will be accorded sovereign authority in certain instances.

The establishment of new supranational episcopal conferences

Council II, *Christus Dominus* (*Decree on the Pastoral Office of Bishops in the Church*), October 28, 1965; (2) ES: Paul VI, *Ecclesiae Sanctae*, Motu Proprio of August 6, 1966: I, n. 41; (3) IL: Sacred Congregation of Rites, Instruction on the Liturgy, Sept. 26, 1964: n. 23.

is tied up with the approval (*approbante*) of the Holy See (CD 38/5). This approval gives them legitimacy, but it is not the source of their basic validity. The bishops themselves constitute these conferences, and the regulations talk only about approval (CD 38/5). It is up to the Holy See to establish "special rules" for these conferences (ES 41/4), but this is not meant to infringe on the right of "each conference . . . to draft its own statutes" (CD 38/3).

We must assume that the general regulations (CD 38) cover supranational conferences as well, and that the "special rules" refer to something beyond this. The *vel territorii* (CD 38/1) and *quaelibet conferentia* (CD 38/3) support that view. Upon the express wish of many conciliar fathers, these provisions, which first referred to national conferences, were made more general.

The regulations governing the statutes of existing episcopal conferences (ES 41/2) are also applicable to supranational conferences. "Review" by the Holy See certainly refers only to legitimacy, not to validity. Mörsdorf inclines to the view that the regulations governing supranational episcopal conferences (ES 41/4) also extend to existing conferences, but he also believes that the new Code of Canon Law should reconsider the difficulties posed to highly desirable international contacts by earlier instructions of the Holy See.

Supranational conferences also should provide for appropriate organisms at various levels (CD 42), for such organisms are often better if they are organized on an international scale.

III
FORM OF ORGANIZATION

The past history of episcopal conferences and the recent conciliar regulations indicate that there are various models for supranational episcopal conferences. Subsequent developments will undoubtedly reveal more.

1. Besides formally established supranational conferences, there will be informal "contacts between episcopal conferences of different nations" (CD 38/5).

2. Besides plenary meetings of bishops (CD 38/2), there should be room for international meetings of an advisory character between delegates to the episcopal conferences. These meetings should provide flexibility and effectiveness.

3. Besides supranational conferences of an advisory character (CD 38/6), such conferences may also have regulatory power in certain cases (IL 23). They could, for example, settle certain pastoral or disciplinary questions (e.g., celibacy) for an area, give the authentic interpretation of decrees passed by international plenary councils, and appoint members and delegates to other international organs of the Church.

4. Quite apart from episcopal meetings of the universal Church, the various branches of the Church must be reorganized on a up-to-date scale. Regional churches must be incorporated into larger international groupings, along cultural, linguistic, political or geographical lines. Such groupings are now provided for by Church law (CD 39-41). Such groupings on a continental or subcontinental level could then be constituted as "patriarchates". One could easily envision episcopal conferences of continental scope for Africa, North America, Latin America, Australia and Europe. One could also envision broad-based groupings for the Arab world and the Far East.

5. Supranational episcopal conferences could also be organized around something other than territorial lines—e.g., according to rite membership. Thus scattered communities would be organized under one competent authority who would have responsibility for their welfare.

6. Ordinarily, supranational episcopal conferences complement national conferences. In cases where they replace national conferences (IL 23) (because the number of bishops is small or for some other legitimate reason), the regulations covering national conferences apply to them.

7. Supranational conferences in the strict sense are to be distinguished from national conferences that include bishops from other lands where no national conference exists (ES 41/3). Such conferences are not affected by the special norms for supranational episcopal conferences.

8. In the Western Church conferences sharing the same rite are the normal case. Interritual conferences are recommended for the Eastern Church (CD 38/6).

9. At present, membership in episcopal conferences is restricted to bishops and persons with episcopal authority (CD 38/2). The inclusion of priests and lay people as experts would not run counter to tradition. On questions that did not affect Church doctrine, they could even be given a deliberative vote.

IV
Their Place in the Church

Only insofar as the Holy See and the local diocese transfer appropriate competence to supranational episcopal conferences will the latter become a real intermediary between diocesan and national conferences on the one hand and the Holy See on the other. All the problems that affect a given area as a whole should be brought before these conferences. In accordance with the principle of subsidiarity, supranational episcopal conferences should enter the picture only to the extent that the welfare of the whole area demands it. On questions of doctrine this will certainly be the case. But it is difficult to say to what extent this would be true in questions of discipline (house Masses, married priests, etc.), especially when the whole episcopate of a region shares pretty much the same view. The member regions of the Church should certainly have some say, through their episcopal conferences at least, about general regulatory norms, important encyclicals and doctrinal statements, and the central synod of bishops. Only then will the gifts and charisms of the Spirit have a chance to work. Only then will believers be able to exchange ideas and mutual aid. Only then will we be able to avoid enslavement to a new legalism (cf. Mt. 23, 4; Gal. 4, 1-5).

An exchange of ideas is also important between various episcopal conferences (CD 38/5) if the growth of the Church and her communities is to be fostered. In the Eastern Church, such an interchange between conferences of different rites would serve the same purpose. An appeals procedure should be limited to questions of the utmost importance.

Supranational conferences are not meant to replace councils. To be sure, we cannot always wait for plenary councils to formulate a binding decision. Less frequent but better prepared international councils will be better able to tackle serious questions of international importance, and, in accordance with the Church's new awareness, they will have a broader base of representation in the whole People of God.

In the conciliar session of November 18, 1965, Paul VI noted that the new vitality of episcopal conferences would contribute greatly to the development and growth of Canon Law. And it is probably the supranational episcopal conferences that can contribute most to the development of a Church unity that shows proper respect for diversity and autonomy within the Church.

For a more extended treatment of this topic, the reader is referred to a forthcoming work on this subject by the present author.

Karl Gastgeber/*Graz, Austria*

Adopting the Life and Ministry of Priests to the Present-Day Pastoral Situation

lthough Vatican Council II's *Decree on the Ministry and Life of Priests* alluded to the fact that in Christ all believers share in a holy and royal priesthood, and "hence there is no member who does not have a part in the mission of the whole body" (n. 2), it also stressed the vital role of the priesthood in the renewal of the Church, and in this connection it spoke of highly important and increasingly difficult tasks.[1] Priests are members of the believing community whom the Lord has appointed to his special service. They share in the ministry of Jesus Christ, the eternal high priest, through which the Church on earth is ceaselessly built up into the People of God, the body of Christ and the temple of the Holy Spirit. The common priesthood, like the particular priesthood, exists to minister to itself as the People of God, and to the world. Insofar as the object of human activity determines the nature of that activity, and insofar as the human situation to which the priestly ministry is directed is historically conditioned and changeable, the ministry and life of priests will have to be determined according to the constantly changing situation within which they are lived.

The purpose of this article is to note the historical development of our theme, particularly its issue in the Code of Canon Law, to demonstrate from the foregoing the consequent theolog-

[1] *Decree on the Ministry and Life of Priests*, n. 1.

ical and canonical principles, to examine these in the light of what the contemporary pastoral situation requires, and in the light of this inquiry to suggest new guiding principles for a *ius condendum*. The extensive nature of this inquiry precludes an exhaustive treatment of all its points.

I

THE MINISTRY AND LIFE OF PRIESTS
FROM THE HISTORICAL AND CANONICAL VIEWPOINT

It appears that in the Church's earliest years there were two constitutions: the Pauline and the Palestinian: "Whereas bishops and deacons most probably originated in Christian communities of Gentile origin, the presbyteral order is of Judaeo-Christian or Jewish origin." [2] In Acts 20, 28-35, presbyters are described as guardians of the flock. Theirs is the leadership of the community and the preservation of orthodoxy.[3] In his own communities, Paul appears to have exercised these functions himself. The function of leadership became a central feature in the structure of the Christian communities, and it is therefore the point from which to launch a consideration of the sacramentality of the presbyteral order. It is also to be observed that with the passing of the Pauline era the constitution in the communities of Gentile origin became separated from the presbyteral constitution, and this led to an obscuring of the precise meanings of the titles *presbyter, episkopos* and *diakonos*.

As time went by the presbyter-bishop combination became dominant at the expense of other charisimatic offices. It is to be assumed that this happened not because of power struggles but because of the precarious situation resulting from the emergence of heretical doctrines.

With a particular order establishing itself in the various com-

[2] Hans Küng, *The Church* (London & New York, 1967), p. 400.
[3] Cf. Hans Küng, *ibid.*, p. 407.

munities, the principle was expanded so that a plurality of bishops led to a monarchical episcopate, and finally the leaders of an individual community became leaders of dioceses. The development had a twofold result: on the one hand the laity became separated from the bishops, and on the other bishops became more distinct from their assistants, among whom were the presbyters. These were chosen by the bishops, and by those bishops they were assigned their duties. The solidarity of a brother among brothers had given way to the rank principle with its accompanying notions of superiority and inferiority, and the consequence was, of course, the emphasizing of hierarchy to the detriment of the notion of service it was supposed to embody. In time the permanence of these developments was further established by the growth of courtly ceremonial and the wearing of distinctive dress. Further developments brought further differentiations and the Code of Canon Law reflects the present position.

Theology sees the hand of God in the hierarchy, which is to say that the hierarchy is of divine institution and embraces the power of orders of bishops, priests and deacons, and the pope's and episcopate's power of jurisdiction. In the course of history, and by virtue of authority divinely conferred, the Church introduced further ranks (Can. 108, §§ 1-3). As a matter of Church order, every priest must belong to a diocese and every religious to an order. The *clericus vagus* is not to be countenanced (Can. 111,§1). The tonsure is the condition of acceptance and incardination (Can. 111,§2). Female clerics seem to have existed only in the Eastern Church (deaconesses). Only clerics may exercise ecclesiastical power (Can. 118). At his own wish, or as a consequence of an ecclesiastical trial, a priest may be laicized. Those in major orders may be readmitted only on the pope's authority, those in minor orders on the bishop's. Because of their station they must lead exemplary lives (Can. 124) and undertake certain spiritual exercises (frequent confession, daily meditation, visits to the blessed sacrament, praying of the rosary and examination of conscience—Can. 125); every three years they must undertake a special retreat in a religious house and they must celebrate Mass frequently every year. All clerics, and particularly priests, must respect and obey their bishop (Can. 127), accept and conscientiously fulfill a job offered them (Can. 128), advance their theological studies (Can. 129), pass the triennial examination by the end of the first three years following ordination and take part in deanery meetings (Cans. 128-31).

The cleric must dress in accordance with the clerical tradition of his region, must refrain from behavior contrary to his station (hunting, gambling, the theatre, etc.), and from other activities that could also be so described (business, medicine, the law, politics—Cans. 138-40). He must live and work within his own diocese (Can. 143). For those in major orders, celibacy and daily praying of the breviary are obligatory. Any form of converse with women to whom suspicion attaches is to be avoided. So as to avoid the accusation of clericalism on account of meddling in matters not their concern, or power seeking, with a view to influencing affairs of state and public life, no cleric may sit in parliament (Can. 138, §4). As regards interior ecclesiastical affairs, all regimentation of the laity by clerics, on the ground that all ecclesiastical power belongs to them, is to be avoided.

Many theologians have adverted to the difficulties that beset the relationship between clergy and laity.[4] The principle of differentiation, as well as the relationship between clergy and laity, constitutes ecclesiastical power as expressed in the powers of order and jurisdiction. The Pseudo-Dionysian-based picture of the Church as a pyramid, with the pope at the top and bishops and priests as middle ranks between God and humanity at large, and who as individuals possessed a grace that enabled them to enlighten the others and make them God-like, has, since J. M. Sailer and J. A. Möhler, been increasingly discredited through the advance of the Pauline view of the Church as the body of Christ. Vatican Council II demonstrated that the old outlook

---

[4] Yves Congar, *Jalon pour une theologie du laicat* (Paris, 1953), pp. 27f.; Karl Rahner, *Schriften zur Theologie* II (Einsiedeln, 1955), pp. 339ff.; Hans Heimerl, *Kirche, Klerus, Laien* (Austria, 1961), pp. 18f.

was outdated, and by the end of the Council the Pauline image of the body of Christ had itself been extended into the view that sees the Church as the People of God journeying through time.

II
THEOLOGICAL AND CANONICAL PRINCIPLES FOR THE PRIESTLY MINISTRY

In the New Testament the word "priest" (*iereus*) is used only for Christ and the People of God (Heb. 4, 14ff.; 1 Pet. 2, 9); alternatively Old Testament and pagan priests are so described. Jesus Christ is the one mediator and high priest, and, like Melchisedech, was called by God. Bearing the sins of the people, he offers himself as expiatory sacrifice. It was his priesthood that ennobled the priesthood that had existed before. Everyone who, through faith, is in Christ shares in his priesthood.

The People of God as a whole, not the hierarchy alone, constitutes the Church. Its members are what they are by virtue of the body of Christ; all are filled with the Spirit and together they possess a special priesthood. This, however, is to be seen not as a priesthood that exists in opposition to the ministerial priesthood, but rather as a state resulting from the establishing of the new covenant, a state characterized by immediate access to God, the offering of spiritual sacrifices to God and the proclamation of his Word (1 Pet. 2, 9; 3, 15).

The building up of Christ's body is the concern of all its members. Preaching and theology,[5] and even the administration of sacraments—baptism, the eucharist, and forgiveness of sins—are part of the responsibility of all believers. Ecclesiastical office is to be seen not as the exercise of authority but as a ministry of service (*diakonia*)[6] whose origin and goal are the following of the Lord in the spirit of love. The diaconal structure of the New Testament communities had no rigid designation of community

[5] Hans Küng, *ibid.*, pp. 375-380.
[6] Karl Heinz Schelkle, *Jüngerschaft und Apostelamt* (Freiburg i. Br., [3] 1965), p. 33.

tasks. The apostle was at once bishop and deacon, prophet and teacher.

In comparison, the nature of ecclesiastical office as it can be observed now is vastly different.[7] One should not attempt to justify these later excesses on the grounds that the arrangements that obtained in the Church's earliest days were primitive. Though the letters Paul wrote to his young communities mentioned no ordinations, this is not the case in the later pastoral letters from which it is clear that office was conveyed through prayer and the imposition of hands. The principle of office in the community is the mission God gave his people, the possession of the necessary charisms and the demands of the actual situation. Where these exist together, there arises an office of community leadership which is creative, suited to the needs of the time and capable of such further development as changing needs might call for.

But as a result of permanent threats from both within (heresies) and without, the exercises of the "pastoral office" became increasingly concerned with ecclesiastical administration. With the onset of the Constantinian era, this purely formal relationship between the official Church and the Church at large became ever more firmly established, reaching its extreme in the Middle Ages through the dominance of the conviction, held also by Boniface VIII, that the clergy were God's sole appointed representatives on earth and the exclusive possessors of ultimate power.

Thus, instead of it being the entire community's task to build up the body of Christ, this function was now reserved to the priest alone, just as he alone could preach the Gospel authoritatively and authentically. The liturgy was his to conduct and control, and he alone could encourage the growth of charismatic gifts within his community. In conjunction with his colleagues he supports his bishop, the communities' rightful leader, in his pastoral functions. The unfolding of the one office of Christ into that of episcopate, presbyterate and diaconate, though thus established by God himself, is subject to the exigencies of history.

[7] Hans Küng, *ibid.*, p. 143.

Thus Vatican Council II restored the diaconate, an office that over the centuries had been reduced to little more than a name The diaconate, quite apart from the ministry it exercises in its own right, will constitute a valuable link between clergy and people, and will serve also as the necessary precursor of a new discipline for a part-time and married priesthood. Essential to ecclesiastical office are God's call to the individual, his response in faith and his acceptance through the Church.

III
Pastoral Action: Present Needs

Reformation, enlightenment, secularization and democratization have brought the Church to the point of crisis. A hierarchy still imprisoned within medieval feudal notions has forfeited the confidence of clergy and people. Local communities see themselves as socially disintegrated groups whose traditional image has become a museum piece. Priests are tired of being cog-like functionaries, and they suffer from the conflict arising from the grinding of democratic freedom and independence against the unquestioning obedience demanded of them by their superiors. Vatican Council II began the process of dispelling the distrust the Church has felt for the world and its secularizing tendencies. It has been recognized that in the Enlightenment and in liberalism, in democracy and in socialism, in the declarations of human rights and in the attempts to establish a community of nations, fundamental Christo-anthropocentric thought-forms have penetrated the human environment. It was Jesus' revelation and proclamation that effected a radical desacralization of the world, thereby creating the conditions in which the sciences could develop. In this connection it is interesting to note that the first Christians were more than once accused of atheism on account of their repudiation of the traditional temple worship with its altars, victim, priests and cultic regulations.

The contemporary secularization process is revealing Christianity's true face. The vanishing patriarchal Church will share her grave with her taboo-surrounded functionaries. Our priests now must be our brothers and fellow human beings, servants of Word and sacrament, guides through religious difficulties. Efforts are being made to simplify and clarify the liturgy and to engage the people in active co-partnership in its celebration.

Those whose office it is to guide the Church must do so in an awareness of the pluralism within human society, and therefore they must show mobility and flexibility with regard to pastoral planning and apostolic activities.[8] Important in this connection is a switch of emphasis from centralized power to control by the local community and its need for a measure of autonomy, from the Christian institution to encounter with the individual Christian, from the representation of factional interests to the well-being of the community, from a ghetto-structured Church to an open Church bent on a worldwide dialogue.

Important changes are taking place in the structure of the local community almost without our noticing the fact. Large city parishes are introducing subsidiary groupings in the residential areas and other large parishes are being broken down into a complex of new, functional groupings. The customary parish-diocese axis needs to be further graduated through the introduction of intermediary pastoral structures such as the deanery. The former geographical concept of the parish will have to be modified in the interests of social structures, and the priest-parish monologue needs to become a dialogue through which the whole community can take part in the process of building Christ's body. As the paternalistic Church disappears, so the patriarchally structured parish will fall from view; the shepherd-flock analogy no longer works and its place is being taken by the community of brothers.

In this basic switch of emphasis, the Church is recovering the form Jesus wished her to have: that which makes known to the world God's self-revelation in Christ. The catastrophic shortage

[8] Norbert Greinacher, "Ändern sich die Strukturen der Seelsorge?" in *Christliche Kunstblätter* 1 (1968), pp. 6-11.

of priests forces the Church to move fast. Just as she has now admitted a married diaconate, and has given full- and part-time lay catechists and female workers in the pastorate a *missio canonica,* so she will now have to turn her attention to a full *and* part-time priesthood, as well as a celibate *and* a married one. The now meaningless minor orders and the subdiaconate should be done away with. Church leadership itself could be enlivened by the institution of elections through appointed electoral bodies and the fixing of a limit to the duration of office. And O. Schreuder's call for professionalism in the priesthood is in keeping with the circumstances of a world in which a man holds his job by virtue of a particular ability. In the search for a new concept of leadership[9] in the ecclesial community, the following factors will have to be considered:

1. The priest must be molded in the spirit of the renewed community which itself will mirror the incarnational and historical essence of the Church: brotherly and collegial, ecumenical and universal, loving and caring. The exercise of his ministry must be a witness to his innermost faith. Thus the socially inhibited solitary, the impersonal official and the crafty diplomat have no place.

2. An independent and full-time leadership can no longer be exercised according to the paternalistic patterns of the past. Instead, a mature and vigorous personality harmoniously combining life-experience and a knowledge of the things of God must be the prerequisite of office. The priest must be a skilled leader and counselor, and his ministry must be characterized by the spirit of service and brotherly concern toward all men. His chief function is the proclamation of the Gospel, and here he must show proper theological competence. What he undertakes in the Spirit in the building up of Christ's body joins him to his bishop and his fellows, and enables him to offer a variegated presbyteral ministry geared to the situation within which he functions.

3. The choice of candidates must be made, and their theologi-

[9] F. Klostermann, "Pastoral-theologische Perspektiven," in *Informationsblatt des Instituts für europäische Priesterhilfe,* 2 (1968), pp. 101f.

cal and spiritual education and further formation undertaken, with the above in mind.

4. The outward appearance of the new leadership must be shorn of its worldly posturings (no more honorary titles, a reform of clerical dress and an outdated way of life). We must also consider Harvey Cox's complaint [10] that a cultic liturgy, the doctrine of distancing oneself from things of the world, the split between the sacral and secular domains, and finally the closed world picture, are the factors that most hinder the Church's mission in the modern world. It is vital that when working for the renewal of the Church we constantly bear in mind that it is Christ's community we are working for and toward, and that this work takes place in time and in a changing society.

IV
TOWARD A IUS CONDENDUM

In what follows I shall attempt to summarize the conclusions reached above in the form of propositions for a new Canon Law.

1. Origin and exemplar of all ecclesiastical office is the eternal high priesthood of Jesus Christ. His total self-surrender in the incarnation and in the paschal mystery prohibits a sacralization of the Christian faith.

2. The Church as a whole must be seen as an *Ekklesia,* that is, as the assembly of all believers of priestly character, the bearer of grace and the mediator of salvation. All Christians belong to the sanctified and sanctifying community of believers who serve God in the Spirit, who offer a spiritual sacrifice and who take part in the forgiveness of sins through faith and love, supplication and reparation.

3. Christ himself gave his Church a body of leaders, and these, as apostles, presbyters and bishops, are charged with the duty of building up the body of Christ and guiding the People of God through the troubles that beset them. Through their ministry

[10] Harvey Cox, *Der Christ als Rebell* (Kassel, 1967), p. 75.

of Word and sacrament they bring about unity and growth in the Church to the extent that they entrust themselves to the guidance of the Spirit. They are responsible for the proper education of the People of God in the faith and for encouraging the maintenance of Christian community life in word and deed. The celebration of the eucharist and the obligation to brotherly love that flows from it are the climax and center of their activity.

4. The diaspora situation necessitates an intensification of the proclamation of the Word in all possible forms: preaching, catechesis, discussion, retreats, house visits and talks on radio and television. The present tension between the Church's traditional teaching and the prophetic interpretation of present and future can do much to invigorate the proclamation of the Gospel.

5. In the exercise of his ministry the officer-holder must be supported by the manifold services of the community. As lay catechists, as leaders in Catholic Action, and as men and women in private and public life, there is much that lay people can do, whether part time or full time, in witness of the faith. The diaconate, in both its married and its celibate form, can contribute much to a loosening up of the clerical state.

6. Brotherly and collegial office in the Church joins bishop and priest in a shared participation in Christ's ministry, and this must be expressed not only through concelebration but also through mutual help in word and deed, through love and obedience, through hospitality and through support in personal difficulty.

7. Ministers must be aware of the danger of clericalism and therefore seek to avoid any form of segregation from the People of God through practicing a spirituality, way of life, prayer or dress peculiar to themselves, or through maintaining separate educational establishments. However appropriate to their role the charism of celibacy might be considered, it should cease to be a condition of ordination. At a time of need the Church is justified in permitting part-time or married priests.

8. Because a measure of freedom is needed if development is to take place, Canon Law must rid itself of petty legislation and

in fact should do no more than lay down general directives whose execution and further specification should be left to national episcopal conferences.

9. In opposition to powerful centralization tendencies, Canon Law needs to stress the principle of subsidiarity. What can be effectively undertaken at a lower level should not be handled at a higher one, and tasks the laity can take on should not be reserved to the clergy.

10. More scope and larger resources should be made available for the spiritual and personal formation and further education of the clergy.

11. A pluriform society requires a pluriform leadership. Thus the shepherd's way of life must be suited to that of his flock; he should not be a remote figure. This would ensure a greater variety of experience among the Church's leadership. The unifying bond is and always will be faith in Christ and selfless love for mankind in the exercise of the ministry.

The above list of points is by no means exhaustive, as its object is only to suggest the kind of reform Canon Law requires in the interests of radical pastoral renewal.

Josef Hornef/*Fulda, West Germany*

Restoring the Diaconate

In view of H. Flatten's comprehensive survey of the diaconate in the light of Canon Law in *Diaconia in Christo* (the standard work on the renewal of the diaconate, edited by Karl Rahner and Herbert Vorgrimler, Freiburg, 1962), a brief summary of the situation is all that is needed here.

With few exceptions theologians were agreed long before Vatican Council II that ordination to the diaconate bore a sacramental character. The publication on November 30, 1947 of Pius XII's statement confirming that the fundamental actions in the rite of ordination to the diaconate were the imposition of hands and the invocation of the Holy Spirit confirmed this view. Ordination confers a particular grace which attaches to the office: it bestows upon the deacon, God's servant, an "indelible seal", a likeness to Christ. The deacon, too, stands *in persona Christi,* as well as *in persona ecclesiae.*[1]

Fundamental to the pre-conciliar diaconate was Can. 973, §1: a candidate may not be ordained to the diaconate unless it is his intention to accept ordination to the presbyterate. This ruling ensured that the diaconate could not amount to more than an intermediate stage preceding sacerdotal ordination. However, there was no corresponding diaconal ministry.

Ordination to the subdiaconate brings with it the obligation to celibacy (Cans. 132 and 949). If a man is still a partner in a

[1] Jean Colson, *La fonction diaconale aux origines de l'Eglise* (Bruges, 1960), p. 79; J. Lecuyer, *Prêtres du Christ—Le sacrement de l'ordre* (Paris, 1957).

valid marriage, Can. 987, §2 forbids him ordination. On the other hand, higher ordination rules out subsequent marriage (Can. 1072).

II

THE POST-CONCILIAR SITUATION

1. *The New Ruling*

The *Constitution on the Church* (n. 29) made two important provisions: it confirmed that the diaconate is a hierarchical rank in its own right, and it opened the door to a married diaconate. Both are of great significance.

(a) The diaconate is no longer merely a milestone along the road to the priesthood, but can itself be a sufficient objective, a lifetime task in which a man can devote himself to the service of God and God's people precisely as a deacon. One becomes a deacon to remain one for life. Thus an office is restored which, ignored these many centuries past, had hitherto been exercised by priests or lay people, when at all.

(b) Reversing a centuries-old tradition, the Council restored a married diaconate, though only for those of mature age. In the priest's case, celibacy is still obligatory, not because the essence of the priestly office demands it but because from many points of view it is desirable (cf. n. 16 of the *Decree on the Ministry and Life of Priests*). But in the case of the diaconate, and for the sake of the pastorate generally, the obligation is dispensed with—except, however, in the case of younger men (see below).

2. *The Nature of the Diaconate*

Chapter III, Article 29, of the *Constitution on the Church* refers to the old- and new-style diaconates and could usefully be made the occasion of an inquiry into the nature of the diaconate. We read: "At a lower level of the hierarchy are deacons, upon whom hands are imposed 'not unto the priesthood, but unto a ministry of service'." At first sight this seems to be an odd statement, for the Council as a whole went out of its way to assure us that the exercise of any office in the Church means service (ministry), and that this includes the papal office, the pope being the *servus servorum Dei*. How, therefore, can it be an emphasis on service that distinguishes a deacon from a priest (and therefore from a bishop)? And when the Constitution goes on to say that the deacon ministers to the People of God through a ministry of liturgy, Word and active charity, are we to take these as the deacon's identification marks? Aren't priests and bishops also called to this threefold ministry? Hasn't the bishop always been regarded as the father of the poor, and did he not in the early Church make use of the diaconate and so ensure that the ministry of service was also undertaken by the hierarchy?

The Constitution also tells us that the source of its own description of the diaconate—not priesthood but ministry of service—was the *Statuta Ecclesiae Antiquae*. Botte and Colson have observed that this view of the diaconate can be traced back to a yet older one in the *Traditio Apostolica* (of Hippolitus?) where we read: "The deacon is ordained not to the presbyterate but to the service of the bishop so that he may do what the bishop instructs." Difficult though it may be to get at the precise meaning of this particular view of the diaconate, it would perhaps have been a more useful text than the present one upon which to base an enquiry into its nature.[2]

The same section of the *Constitution on the Church* stresses that the deacon exercises his threefold ministry *in communion with the bishop and his presbyters*.[3] Thus, though ecclesiastical office is conferred through the sacrament of orders at three different levels, it is seen to be a unity. Within this one office stands the

[2] Jean Colson would like to see the text interpreted in this way: "Le diacre n'est pas ordonné à fonction *sacerdotale* de l'Evêque mais a la fonction *diaconale* de l'Evêque." Even if this interpretation is correct, I would not like to see it absolutized. The episcopal *diaconia* is transmitted not only to the deacon but also to the priest (*Decree on the Ministry and Life of Priests*, n. 6); cf. Colson, *op. cit.*, pp. 97ff.; also B. Botte, "Das Weihesakrament nach den Gebeten des Weiheritus," in J. Guyot, *Das apostolische Amt* (Mainz, 1961).

[3] Cf. also the *Constitution on the Church*, n. 28: "These [the bishops] in their turn have legitimately handed on to different individuals in the Church various degrees of participation in this ministry. Thus the divinely

deacon, the possessor of the *tertium gradum sacri ordinis*.[4] The deacon is not a priest in the narrower sense (he is not a priest of the sacrifice, if one wants to put it that way), yet he exercises a priestly office of service. The *Decree on the Apostolate of the Laity* (n. 2) stresses that lay people, too, by virtue of the common priesthood, share in their own way in the priestly, prophetic and royal ministry of Christ; and if that can be said of lay people generally, it can certainly be said of the deacon as an ordained officeholder of the Church. The deacon belongs to the official priesthood (as distinct from the common priesthood of all believers). As Pius XII put it, he is "of the priesthood".

This is important with regard to the deacon's position in the community. He is not a priest's stand-in, or the parish priest's personal servant, there to do his bidding; neither is he the parish's jack-of-all-trades. He is the parish priest's colleague, and together they minister to the needs of the community. But this sharing in the priesthood—using this word in its wider sense—will also affect the deacon's spirituality. Priest and deacon assist the bishop in fulfilling the Church's ministry of service (*Constitution on the Church*, n. 20). But a deacon is no more a pale copy of a priest than a priest is a sort of inferior version of a bishop. In other words, the object of the deacon's office is not simply that of assistant; it has its own characteristics.

What then is the "nature peculiar to this order" of which Pope Paul speaks in the Motu Proprio *Sacrum diaconatus ordinem*"? (Article 41 of the *Constitution on the Church* speaks of deacons "sharing in the mission and grace of the supreme priest in their own special way".) What in fact makes a deacon a deacon? The answer, I suggest, is service, priestly service at all levels of his office: the diaconate of the liturgy of the Word and of active charity, teaching, sanctifying and leading in all he does *ex officio*.

But the particular form of service offered by bishop, priest and

---

established ecclesiastical ministry is exercised on different levels by those who from antiquity have been called bishops, priests and deacons."

[4] Pope Paul VI, Motu Proprio *Sacrum diaconatus ordinem* of June 18, 1967.

deacon is not the same. In the bishop's case his primary concerns are the exercise of his teaching office, the maintenance of ecclesiastical office through the sacrament of holy orders and the administration of his diocese. The priest will regard the celebration of the eucharist and the administration of the sacraments as his primary function and duty. The deacon, however, starting from the altar as the focus of the local worshiping community, will see his primary function in responding to his fellow men in physical or spirtual need: a sacramental and liturgical ministry, and a ministry of service, to his fellow men—the ministry of the Word and the ministry of love working in close harness. The ministry of service is also the proclamation of the Lord through action, and that naturally entails the proclamation of the Word.

The deacon is one who undertakes necessary works of social welfare in the spirit proper to his office. He should not regard this type of work as his own exclusive domain, but should encourage others in the community to undertake it also. In this way, the "Church of the poor", a concept given considerable stress during Vatican Council II, can become a reality. The importance of this for the role of the Church in the Third World is undeniable. The deacon's missionary role is also important: his work among those alienated from the Church as also his introduction of new members to her and his supervision of their catechumenate. This is precisely the area in which the deacon could exercise his office independently.

The foregoing should give us some idea of what characterizes the office and role of the diaconate. The deacon should personify the notion of service, and this he will do by dedicating himself to God and to God's people through developing his ministry of service within the specific diaconal duties allotted to him. In all this, however, his approach to his work will be strongly influenced by his particular environment. Thus it may sometimes be necessary for a deacon to concentrate on one particular function. But even here, whatever and wherever his particular role, a deacon must ensure that the exercise of his ministry proceeds from the liturgy as the focus of the priestly state.

3. Necessity of the Diaconate

The duties proper to a deacon are best examined in the light of the relevant Motu Proprio. Vatican Council II expressly says that in many parts of the Church it would be difficult to fulfill these necessary duties without the diaconate. For this reason the Council wished to reestablish the diaconate as "a proper and permanent rank of the hierarchy" (*Constitution on the Church,* n. 29). It did not decree that the diaconate should immediately be restored everywhere, but left this decision to the national episcopal conferences who are to reach their decision in the light of requirements within their territories. Should an episcopal conference decide in favor of introducing the diaconate, then final permission has to be obtained from the Apostolic See.

III

THE DEACON IN THE LIGHT OF THE MOTU PROPRIO[5]

1. General Observations

In the Motu Proprio *Sacrum diaconatus ordinem* the pope expanded the Council's conclusions by setting out more detailed regulations. These basic regulations establish an overall framework, certain aspects of which can be further expanded by an episcopal conference or local ordinary.

The Motu Proprio first stresses that Canon Law—insofar as it is not hereby altered or extended—applies in full to the restored diaconate. Also applicable until further notice are all regulations concerning ordination to the diaconate and the stages that precede such ordination.

2. Age, Marriage and Remarriage

No one may be ordained a deacon until he has reached his twenty-fifth year, and then only if he accepts a permanent obliga-

[5] Herbert Vorgrimler, Introduction to and Commentary on the Motu Proprio *Diaconia Christi: Documentation* 6/7 (Freiburg i. Br., 1967);

tion to celibacy (n. 5); an episcopal conference may insist upon a higher minimum age. A married man, the *vir grandioris aetatis* (the "man of more mature age") can be ordained when he has completed his thirty-fifth year (n. 12). This in most cases will also mean that the prospective deacon's marriage will already be of some years' standing (n. 13). His wife must agree to his ordination (n. 11). After he has received orders, a deacon may not marry (n. 16) even if admitted at a more mature age and therefore even if he is widowed after ordination. Archbishop Cornelis of Elizabethville, and others, protested vehemently against this particular condition, maintaning that in Africa's case (and I would say elsewhere also) it would create a grievous obstacle.[6] Responsible authorities in Rome responded with the assurance that they would be generous with dispensations in such cases.[7] But a firm ruling to suit their case would have been better.

3. The Deacon's Formation

The formation of the younger candidate is to take place in a special college. It will last three years (n. 9) and be followed by a period of practical training (n. 10). Curriculum and discipline are to be determined by the bishops who maintain the college.

The married candidate, who will usually also have a civil profession, also has to undergo a basic training program and should also spend a while in a special college. If that is not possible, then, in accordance with pre-Tridentine custom, he should attach himself to an experienced priest and receive suitable training at his hands (nn. 14 and 15). The episcopal conferences are responsible for establishing the details of the basic training program a married candidate must undergo.

J. Hornef, "Die römische Ausführungsbestimmungen zu den Diakonatsbeschlüssen des Konzils. Eine kritische Betrachtung der jetzigen Rechtslage," in *Heiliger Dienst* 21 (1967), pp. 109ff.

[6] "Le diaconat au Congo-Léo," in P. Winninger-Y. Congar, *Le diacre dans l'Eglise et le monde aujourd'hui* (Paris, 1966), pp. 239ff. On the theological aspects, see St. Lyonnet, "Le diacre, 'mari au seul femme,'" *ibid.*, pp. 272ff.

[7] *Diaconia Christi*, pp. 59ff.

4. *The Deacon's Duties*

The duties foreseen for the deacon in the Motu Proprio are more extensive than the Council itself was able to specify. Ultimately, however, it is a question of which of the permitted duties the bishop assigns him (n. 22). The following areas are listed:

The deacon is expected to assist bishop or priest in the celebration of the liturgy. (This refers primarily to the eucharist, particularly when celebrated in the form of a *missa cum diacono.*) He can administer baptisms, distribute communion and take viaticum to the dying. In the absence of a priest he can assist at the sacrament of matrimony. He can preside at burial rites. He can instruct and exhort the people, and this will mean taking religion lessons (there is no direct reference to preaching, probably because in the granting of this faculty note will have to be taken of the individual deacon's ability). In the absence of a priest (*religiosi cultus officiis*) he can preside at church services and lead pilgrimages. Leading during the liturgy of the Word is a particular diaconal function (especially when no priest is available; cf. also the *Constitution on the Sacred Liturgy*, n. 35).

The deacon, operating in the name of the hierarchy, may perform administrative duties and undertake works of social welfare (the ministry of service and love). As a representative of the parish priest or bishop he can minister to the needs of remote communities, since by virtue of his ordination he shares in the pastoral office. He should also offer his support to the lay apostolate.

Whatever his task, and they are clearly extensive, a deacon is under the authority of the bishop and of the priest who preside over the care of souls in the area in which he is working (n. 23).

5. *Duties of the Episcopal Conference and the Local Ordinary*

The episcopal conference and the local ordinary must determine the *honesta sustentatio*, the annual income appropriate to the family circumstances of the full-time deacon (n. 20). The part-time deacon should, as far as possible, maintain himself and his family on the income he receives from his civil profession (n. 21). It is for episcopal conferences to ensure that the cultivation of the spiritual life, on which Pope Paul lays so much stress, is properly provided for. This aspect should be supervised by the local ordinary (n. 26). It is for the episcopal conference to decide on suitable diaconal apparel (n. 31). (When not taking part in the liturgy he should dress like anyone else!)

Once an episcopal conference's recommendation to restore the diaconate in its territory has found papal approval, the ultimate decision to implement the recommendation lies with the local ordinary (n. 3), for it was always intended that a bishop should have the last word in his own diocese. (The restored diaconate will only thrive if given freedom, and it must not be overlooked that circumstances might differ materially even between adjacent dioceses.) Wherever possible, and for reasons of expediency, dioceses will pool their resources when arranging for the formation of their deacons.[7] Even where a bishop decides that for the time being he does not wish to introduce the diaconate in his own diocese, he must ensure that ordination candidates in his diocese are placed elsewhere. He can either release them from further pursuit of their goal (Cans. 955 and 958) or, with permission from the bishop concerned, ordain them for another diocese so that they can be incardinated there (Can. 969, §2).

IV

DE LEGE FERENDA

Canon Law, as it at present stands, still awaits adjustment in the light of the conciliar decisions affecting the diaconate and the Motu Proprio wholly devoted to it. With this in mind I beg the support of the national episcopal conferences, wherever they feel able to offer it, in urging the following recommendations upon the competent authorities in Rome.

[7] *Diaconia Christi*, pp. 59ff.

1. That if it is not considered appropriate to authorize local ordinaries to decide for themselves whether or not a man is sufficiently mature for ordination, could it not at least be agreed that the minimum age at ordination for a married man be reduced to thirty?

2. That deacons widowed after ordination be permitted to remarry—if not of their own accord, then at least with their bishop's authority.

3. That deacons be authorized, by virtue of powers conferred at ordination, to administer the anointing of the sick (with the agreement of the bishop or parish priest).

4. That it might be more appropriate if one or other of the minor orders (lector, acolyte), and the subdiaconate (which could resume its former character as a minor order), be reserved as preliminary steps to the full diaconate, in which case the full diaconate would become the sole preliminary step in ordination to the presbyterate.

5. That it might be appropriate to create a new order for women who work for the Church (though it is not recommended that the sacramental diaconate be extended to them).

6. That it should be made easier for a deacon to revert to the lay state.

7. That authorizing the parish community to elect a candidate and recommend their choice to their bishop is a step worth considering.

8. That a deacon be permitted to receive communion under both kinds in every *missa cum diacono*.

9. That it might be useful to stress the exceptional character of the measures through which a layman is authorized to administer communion and to preach.

Finally, let us all take to heart what Congar said at the Congress on the Diaconate in Rome in 1965: "Enough has been said and written about the diaconate, and we should now get on with its realization! Any further points will come to light through experience."

PART II
BIBLIOGRAPHICAL
SURVEY

Petrus Huizing, S.J./*Nijmegen, Netherlands*

On the Administration of Justice in the Church

On August 15, 1967 Pope Paul VI published the Apostolic Constitution *Regimini Ecclesiae universae*. This became operative on March 1, 1968. This Constitution contains a new statute for the Roman curia. It will be more clearly determined by general regulations (*ordo*) and special ones to be drafted by each organ of the curia. The pope had already announced a reform of the curia on September 23, 1963. Immediately a commission had been set up to study the preparation for this reform. This commission consisted of the curial cardinals Roberti, Jullien and Albareda. The last two died and were replaced by Heard and Forni. The secretary was the auditor of the Rota, Giovanni Maria Pinna. Later on two members of the Secretariate of State, Dell'Acqua and Martin, were added. The pope himself was personally and closely involved in the preparation of the Constitution.

How far does the Constitution accept the principle of the "separation of powers"? Most States accept in general that the "powers" or competencies in legislative, executive and judicial matters are vested in separate bodies. Does the Constitution allot particularly the administration of justice to independent bodies, distinct from those charged with legislative and executive powers? Does the Constitution accept an "administrative jurisdiction", i.e., an independent juridical body accessible to anyone who feels that his rights are interfered with by a particular act of the authority?

An answer to these questions was expected from the Constitution,[1] and it was obvious that these questions would be presented for consideration. They were asked long before the Constitution. The last important reorganization of the curia took place in 1908, under Pius X. One of the aims of his Constitution *Sapienti consilio* was precisely the separation of government and justice. Justice in decisions on conflicts between various rights within the ecclesial community was almost wholly in the hands of the cardinalitial congregations. The Rota, originally destined to deal with justice, busied itself till 1870 with civil processes in the Papal States, and afterward with the processes of beatification and canonization. Pius X wanted to restore it to its original function. This was prevented by a development which he could hardly foresee. For since that time the number of matrimonial processes has increased considerably. The Rota, like most diocesan tribunals, is almost exclusively occupied with these cases. In 1908, 8 of the 17 processes of the Rota were matrimonial cases; in 1957, 257 out of the 259! Proper disputes about rights within the Church's community do not go to the tribunals but are dealt with by the cardinalitial congregations, through administrative channels (*per viam administrativam*). An appeal against a decision of a congregation is lodged with the same congregation. All one can do is to ask for a new investigation. It is no longer possible to go to a tribunal, not even the Rota.

Moreover, on September 15, 1917, after the promulgation of the new Code of Canon Law, Pope Benedict XV charged the cardinalitial congregations with its execution and, where necessary, to give the required instructions. The intention was to separate the legislative from the executive or administrative func-

[1] A. Gommenginger, "Reform der kirchlichen Rechtsprechung," in *Orientierung* 32 (1968), pp. 25-27; also cf. *ibid.*, "Verfassung und Strukturen in einem neuen Kirchenrecht," in *Orientierung* 31 (1967), pp. 25-28; J. Neumann, "Gesamtkirchliches Grundgesetz," in *Theologie im Wandel* (Munich, 1967), pp. 415-49; for further literature, see *Concilium* 8 (1965), pp. 50ff.

tions. Legislation for the Church as a whole would then be reserved to the pope. The curial administrative bodies would then not have any legislative function in normal circumstances. A vast number of compulsory canonical norms were published by the cardinalitial congregations. It has even been queried whether practically the sole independent jurisdiction in matrimonial matters did not fall within the administrative competence of the congregation of the sacraments. And although the commission for the interpretation of Canon Law rejected a direct dependence of the diocesan and metropolitan tribunals on this congregation, jurisdiction in matrimonial matters is nevertheless under the control of the congregation of the sacraments.[2]

In their writings the canonists have busied themselves for years with the problems of this "separation of powers", of an independent jurisdiction and of an administrative jurisdiction. Before their annual meeting in 1966 at Pittsburgh, the Canon Law Society of America organized a three-day seminar on the revision of Canon Law. Thirty-five experts in very different fields took part. In the resolutions special attention was paid to the "separation of the powers". They recommended that the pope and the bishops should use separate bodies for the functions of legislation, administration and justice. They pointed to the need for an independent judicial body to which any member of the Church could turn for the protection of his rights.

It was also argued that because of the massive violations of the most elementary human rights during the last decades, people have become very sensitive about real or supposed arbitrary conduct by the authorities. Inviolable human rights have been the subject of a Declaration by the United Nations in 1948 and also by the Council of Europe in 1950. Vatican Council II emphasized the dignity of the human person and the personal rights that are therein implied; it maintained that these rights may be violated by any authority, whether civil or ecclesiastical.

For the members of the Council of Europe there exists a tribunal, accessible to anyone who feels that his human rights have

2 *AAS* 32 (1940), p. 317.

been infringed by the authority. The question has been raised whether a similar body should not be set up in the Church. While it is true that the Church cannot be equated with a democratic State, it is nevertheless a community where there can be no room for arbitrariness, even for apparently religious motives. It has been observed that many far-reaching decisions are taken in the Church through complicated and secret administrative channels against which there is no appeal. It should be possible for anyone who feels that his rights are infringed by measures of government to be able to appeal to a higher tribunal. The comprehensive protection of rights is a necessary implication of the recognition that there is true justice within the Church. One can no longer talk of a judicial order when the existing norms and their application cannot be maintained and controlled by an independent judiciary.

It was therefore obvious that after the reorganization of the Roman curia, the question would be raised as to how far these requirements were taken into account in this reorganization. Article 1 of the Constitution *Regimini* says: "The Roman curia . . . consists of congregations, tribunals, offices and secretariates." Judicial and administrative functions therefore remain separated in principle. Article 7 states: "Questions which demand judicial investigation must be referred to the competent tribunals." The Constitution does not define these questions any further. On the basis of Article 12 one has to assume that the definitions of the present Code will remain valid unless the general regulations state otherwise. According to Article 39 the congregation of the faith has "a twofold procedure: either administrative or judicial, according to the nature of the matter to be dealt with." This congregation therefore has administrative and judicial functions within its own competence.

The congregation for the sacraments is competent in all that concerns the regulations of the seven sacraments, "with the reservation . . . of the Apostolic Signature with regard to prolongation of competence in relevant judicial matters and also with regard to the control of the administration of justice in relevant judiciary matters and the setting up of regional and interregional tribunals" (Art. 54). Thus the organization of the judiciary passes into the hands of a judiciary authority. The congregation of the sacraments remains exclusively competent to deal with the investigation of whether a marriage is ratified, which is not strictly a judicial function (Art. 56). It also judges the obligations attached to the higher sacred orders and investigates questions about their validity or refers these to a competent tribunal (Art. 57). It is therefore the congregation which judges whether the judiciary will operate in these matters.

The judicial section of the congregation of rites is charged with the "processes concerning the servants of God" (Art. 62), and there must be very few who would insist here on an "independent judiciary". The congregation for the clergy has to "judge conflicts about precedence among the clergy, excepting the right of the congregation of the religious to judge matters of precedence among religious; it also deals through the administrative channels with other differences between the clergy, between the clergy and the laity, or between diocesan and religious clergy (Art. 68). Here, too, Article 7 will remain in force, in that questions which require a judicial investigation must be referred to the competent tribunal.

The congregation for the religious covers all that relates to religious institutes of the Latin rite "apart from the competence . . . of the tribunals where a judicial procedure is required" Art. 73). The congregation for the propagation of the faith "refers matrimonial cases and other matters that require judicial procedure to the Sacred Roman Rota" (Art. 87). Insofar as the Rota is concerned the norms of the Code of Canon Law remain valid. But its competence is extended to processes of declaration of nullity of marriages between Catholics and non-Catholics and marriages of non-Catholic baptized persons (Art. 109).

And so, with the exception of the competence of the Apostolic Signature to deal with matters concerning judiciary organization, there is no change in the Constitution regarding the relations between government and the judiciary. Nor is the principle expressed that for legislation or the preparation of legislation a body must be set up distinct from the organs of government. It has been mentioned that the episcopal synod as representing the bishops of the world might be suited for this function. All government, that of the Church included, is supposed to be inclined to uniformity and centralization. Because of its composition the episcopal synod would therefore have a better understanding of the differences in the solution of problems, according to the needs and requirements of the various cultural regions. One may indeed expect that the influence of the episcopal synod is going to be more decisive than that of the curial bodies, at least in basic issues, including those that concern Church order. In that case the function of the curial organs would obviously become more limited to execution or administration.

The Constitution has taken account of the demand for an organ for the administrative judiciary, for this jurisdiction is handed over to the highest ecclesiastical tribunal, the Apostolic Signature. This has two sectors. The first has the necessary powers already assigned to the Signature by Canon Law and the competence to deal with the organization of the judiciary. "In the second sector the Apostolic Signature decides differences that have arisen out of an act of ecclesiastical government and of which it has been made cognizant by an appeal against a decision taken by a competent curial authority, whenever it is claimed that this decision has violated some law. In these cases the Signature decides either whether the appeal should be allowed or on the illegality of the contested action" (Art. 106). "This same sector deals with conflicts about competence between various organs of the Apostolic See in such matters of government as have been referred to it by the congregations of the Roman curia, and investigates matters committed to it by the pope" (Art. 107).

It should be noted here that if one thinks oneself unjustly treated by other bodies than those of the curia, one cannot turn directly to the Signature but only to the competent congregation.

Only after this congregation has given its decision can the Signature be appealed to. The Constitution could clearly not deal with administrative justice at the diocesan, provincial or regional level. It has also been objected that the judges of the Signature are cardinals who are also members of congregations. The members of an administrative tribunal should indeed have experience of government, but they should not belong to the government as judges. No secular constitutional law would allow ministers to function as administrative judges.

Nevertheless, one can only rejoice at the introduction of the principle of administrative justice into the organization of the Church. It opens the way toward further development in this direction. Moreover, we shall have to see how the episcopal synod, the cardinalitial congregations, the Rota and the Signature are going to function in the future. Law can indeed create organs of justice, but the actual course of events is often determined by factors that lie outside the law, at least outside the written law.

The conference of the *officiales* (the men entrusted with the bishop's jurisdiction in an episcopal court) of Germany, in Bonn, April 13-15, 1966, drafted a number of suggestions for the revision of the Code's judicial procedure in matrimonial cases. Representatives of the *officiales* of Austria, Switzerland, Luxemburg, Denmark, Sweden and Norway gave their cooperation.[3] The well-known canonist Scheuermann, of Munich, provided a careful commentary.[4] Here I shall mention only a few of the main changes that have been suggested.

Most dioceses have to contend with serious shortages in the personnel available for their tribunals. Often the *officialis* is neither released from his ordinary duties (e.g., as vicar general) nor adequately trained in Canon Law. Usually these same difficulties hold for the rest of the personnel, such as the diocesan

---

[3] *Archiv für katholisches Kirchenrecht* 136 (1967), pp. 40-45.

[4] A. Scheuermann, "Vorschläge zum kirchlichen Eheprozeszrecht," *ibid.*, pp. 3-45; H. Flatten, "Die freie Beweiswürdigung im kanonischen Prozesz," in *Theol. Quart. Schr.* 139 (1959), pp. 427ff., esp. pp. 454-60.

judges, the examining judges, the promoter of justice (*promotor iustitiae*) and the defender of the matrimonial tie (*defensor vinculi*). It is suggested that courses should be organized by the episcopal conferences for all who have a function to fulfill in the administration of justice and are not adequately trained for it. Scheuermann thinks that lay people could not be appointed as ecclesiastical judges. According to him the jurisdiction of ecclesiastical judges cannot be severed from ordination. A layman could be appointed as clerk of the court, possibly as a *defensor vinculi,* and, if necessary, as an advisor to the judge with a consultative voice.

According to Gommenginger, however, lay people, such as lawyers trained in Canon Law, could very well make up for the lack of canonically trained priests. Some universities, like those of Munich and Strasbourg, have incorporated an institute for Canon Law in their theological faculty, where lay people, women included, are registered as students. This happens, moreover, in other faculties of Canon Law. Gommenginger considers as outdated the opinion that only a priest can function as a judge, *defensor vinculi* or *promotor iustitiae.* In actual fact, even according to the present law, jurisdiction can be granted to any cleric. And since one becomes a cleric through the reception of the tonsure, the formality of this tonsure would be enough to grant jurisdiction to lay people! Few would support this point of view today.

Those who are the culpable and deliberate cause of the nullity of their marriage, including non-Catholics, are not entitled themselves to bring an action for declaration of nullity to the ecclesiastical tribunal. They may bring this declaration of nullity to the *promotor iustitiae* who can then institute proceedings if he thinks it in the interest of public order. It is suggested to drop these limitations of the ability to institute proceedings for a declaration of nullity. Not only the *promotor iustitiae,* but any interested Catholic should be able to institute proceedings for a declaration of nullity.

The questions that must be put to the parties, witnesses and experts must be drafted by the *defensor vinculi* and deposited with the clerk of the court in a sealed envelope. The judge may only open the envelope at the actual session. The point of this is to ensure that the declarations then given cannot be prepared in a way that would be deceitful. This system has many disadvantages. It is not right that the *defensor vinculi,* himself a party to the process, should draft the questions. Moreover, usually he is not yet sufficiently familiar with the matter, and therefore he will be likely to draft his questions on the basis of fixed patterns. The result would be that the ensuing declarations would give a false picture of the real situations that are constantly changing. The suggestion, therefore, is that the judge himself draft these questions and thus be able to adjust them constantly to the concrete situation during the session. Moreover, often enough the witnesses or experts must be informed beforehand of the points on which they have to make their declarations.

In processes for a declaration of nullity of marriage, the declarations of the parties are not accepted by themselves as proof, not even when the judge is personally fully convinced of their sincerity, and therefore of the nullity of the marriage. Canonists such as Flatten and Dordett, as well as the Canon Law Society of America, have already pointed out the need to attach more value to the declarations of the parties. We might add that this holds particularly for the many countries where an ecclesiastical process can only be of interest for the ecclesiastical status of the parties. There the property rights and other civil consequences of a broken marriage have usually already been settled by the civil court, and the danger of deceit in matrimonial cases is far less there than in a country like Italy, for instance.

The *defensor vinculi* is always obliged to appeal against a decision given in the first court when this decision is in favor of nullity, even if this decision is based on irrefutable proof and even if the *defensor vinculi* wholly agrees with this proof. The parties must then still wait for a useless process and decision from a second court. It is therefore suggested that in such cases the *defensor vinculi* be no longer obliged to appeal. Scheuermann does not think it safe to leave the decision to the *defensor vinculi*, either in the first or in the second instance (in the judicial sense). Neither the first court nor the bishop can make this decision, since no one can be judge in his own interests. Hence he wants this obligation to appeal to remain, but the second court should be able to decide on a motion proposed by the *defensor vinculi* of the second court whether the proceedings should be taken further or not. In all cases, moreover, a shorter procedure is desirable in the second instance.

Many objections have been made to the Rota as the third instance for the whole world. Spain has its own third instance, the Rota of the nunciature of Madrid. The Signature can delegate jurisdiction in the third instance to local tribunals in special cases. An appeal to the Roman Rota implies the necessity to provide a difficult and expensive translation of all the documents of the case into Latin, Italian or French. Such translations reproduce rarely, if ever, all the subtleties of the original. Moreover, a correct assessment of the documents demands an understanding of the opinions and customs of the various countries or regions. To deal with appeals from all countries of the world within a reasonable time is impossible. Hence papal exhortations about speeding up the procedure have no effect. The Roman lawyers' knowledge of foreign languages is naturally limited. This often makes it difficult to correspond with them. It has also been discreetly pointed out—without being too specific about this—that the fees they ask are out of all proportion with the work that is asked of them. This is a fact which seriously worries even several judges of the Rota. Many therefore feel that it is a matter of urgency to decentralize this administration of justice in the third instance. This third level of justice should have its own tribunal for every extensive linguistic region.

Scheuermann thinks that it is impossible to delegate the competence to dissolve marriages which are not ratified or not wholly Christian *in favorem fidei* (in the interest of the Christian party) to bishops or episcopal conferences. On the other hand, the Canon Law Society of America, at its annual meeting of 1967 at Denver, accepted a documented advisory paper to the American bishops in which they recommend the bishops to ask the pope to enable them to dissolve marriages *in favorem fidei*. Even if it is thought that this competence is linked with the papal primacy, it still does not exclude delegation. Here, too, decentralization would considerably reduce the length of the procedure and the high expenses involved. In a vast majority of the cases a speedy decision is important for those concerned. The requirements for these dissolutions are well known and can be judged in many countries with certainly no less expertise than in Rome. Here, too, the decisive factor for the organization of justice should not be the traditional rights of particular authorities but the obvious interests of the members of the Church. The same arguments plead in favor of a decentralization of processes and procedures connected with the validity of the higher orders and religious vows, and the duties connected with these, as well as the dispensation from these duties. In all these cases it is a matter of situations which can only be properly judged by those who are personally in contact with those involved. It is not exactly an ideal situation, particularly in an ecclesial community, that those who have to give the final decision in such far-reaching human problems are people who know nothing whatever about the persons concerned and who judge purely on the basis of documents and dossiers. This very serious difficulty cannot be overcome by even the most expert specialized knowledge.,

This leads naturally to the question whether, particularly for these profoundly personal problems of married people, or of religious and priests, judicial treatment by judges and tribunals in official processes is really the best procedure. Where genuine judicial disputes are concerned, we all like to see a kind of justice that is well organized, objective and legally well qualified, even in an ecclesial community, not only for the sake of the claimant, but also for the sake of peace and good order in the community. When, for instance, there is a conflict between a bishop and a parish priest about the legitimacy of a transfer or a dismissal, it is highly desirable that they can take this conflict to an ecclesiastical judicial body which is recognized and accepted by the faithful as able to provide impartial and expert justice. Otherwise there will never be a solution to a judicial conflict that is satisfactory either to the parties concerned, or to the community. Insofar as the personal problems, mentioned above, are concerned, the various proposals for a better and speedier procedure are valuable. A more basic revision is probably unattainable in the near future. And then it is only sensible to be patient and to support those improvements which can be brought about now. Nevertheless, one can and must even now ask whether all those processes of marriage and sacred orders and all those procedures should not be replaced by a far more personal and pastoral approach. In sacramental theology, one hopes, some thought will be given to the question whether the existential "validity" and "non-validity" of the sacraments can really coincide with juridically fixed norms —in other words, whether this existential "validity" or "non-validity" can be juridically determined at all. And even if that were possible, would it be really important for a believing community? Is it not far more important to give people who are saddled with these personal problems all the help possible so that they can reach a decision that is personal and justified, and personally justified in such a way that the ecclesial community can accept it?

Ivan Žužek, S.J./*Rome, Italy*

The Sacramental Canon Law of the Christian East

I

THE NEED OF A MORE ADEQUATE SACRAMENTAL THEOLOGY

The sacraments, as signs that combine a human gesture and the divine Word, have the "structure of him whose grace they efficiently dispense" (Crespel 7).[1] They are therefore necessarily humble, simple and scandalous for many, as was Christ himself garbed in human nature (*cf. ibid.*). The Canon Law on the sacraments belongs to the most humble part of the human contribution to the way in which the grace of God is administered to his people. It can do little more than apply the theology on the sacraments to actual life. Imperfections of the canons in this connection reflect the deficiencies of a theology which was too much inclined to separate the seven sacraments from the root sacrament, the Church, and from Christ, treating them as "things" (*C.I.C., De rebus,* Can. 726) that operated automatically, almost independently of the faith of those who received them (cf. *ibid.* 9).

The realization in the Catholic Church of the need of a much deeper Christocentric theology on the sacraments is a good sign for Orientals, Catholic and Orthodox, that their theological opinions will now be taken into consideration. Consequently, they have good reason to hope that their discipline in administering the sacraments will henceforward be respected. The will to "Latinize" the Orientals in this regard was due mainly to an

---

[1] "Ont en eux-mêmes la structure de Celui dont ils distribuent . . . la grace. . . ." The page references in brackets refer to the works listed in the bibliography at the end of the article. The bibliography is divided under the same headings as the article itself.

inability to listen carefully to the great voice of Oriental theologians and a tendency to a self-sufficient monologue. There never was a real dialogue or a respect for the "legitimate variety in the theological expression of doctrine" (*Decree on Ecumenism,* n. 17) with regard to the Christian East. Still less has the West been ready to admit that sometimes the Oriental tradition has come nearer than the Western "to an apt appreciation of certain aspects of a revealed mystery, or has expressed them in a clearer manner" (*ibid.*).

For a new code on the sacraments, a new approach to an "ecumenical theology" is particularly essential. The treatises of so-called Oriental theology on the sacraments that have been produced up until now are occasionally of great worth (Jugie, De Vries, Spačil), but some authors engage in a certain type of comparative theology, which accentuates differences.

The *Decree on Ecumenism* (n. 13) disapproves such theology. Articles 5 and 6 of the *Decree on Catholic Churches of the Eastern Rite,* and, still more, articles 14-17 of the Decree on *Ecumenism* insist on the legitimate variety of theological traditions, declaring that the "entire heritage" of Eastern "spirituality and liturgy, of discipline and theology, in their various traditions, belongs to the full catholic and apostolic character of the Church" (n. 17).

Chrysostomus, in a recent article, opposes Schultze, who is not favorable to two theologies, Eastern and Western. Chrysostomus (p. 41), while recognizing that one cannot, as Schultze says (p. 78), "neglect a thousand years of theological evolution",[2] sees no reason why this evolution should be proclaimed as a model for Oriental theology.

In the actual Code of Eastern Canon Law the section on seminaries is still missing. This is fortunate, since it would have contained the Latin Can. 1366, §2, that imposes the teaching of the doctrine of St. Thomas Aquinas, as happened with Can. 589, §1 of the Latin Code, in which there is question of the education of religious. For Oriental religious (Motu Proprio *Postquam apostolicis,* Can. 128) the doctor *par excellence* is St. Thomas. To

[2] "Eine tausendjährige theologische Entwicklung überspringen."

make this more acceptable, however, the canon adds that St. John Damascene was his predecessor.

Orientals have the greatest esteem for St. Thomas, who cannot be ignored in any theology, yet they feel more at ease with their own way of expressing the truths of divine revelation. The late Patriarch Maximos IV, in the central commission of Vatican Council II, underlined a few points in this respect that express very well the feeling of Orientals about Thomism, notwithstanding the altogether exceptional greatness of Aquinas.

1. Thomistic systematization cannot be said to be universal in the Church. The East has another theological system which should not be excluded from Catholic ways of thinking.

2. Thomistic terminology is not always conformable with that of the Oriental Churches, particularly in regard to the sacraments (*materia, forma, ex opere operato*).

3. There is a danger that involuntarily more weight will be given to the doctrine of St. Thomas than to the collective thinking of the Fathers of the Church.

4. St. Thomas was subject to the prejudices of his time with regard to Orientals and should be used in the dialogue with the Orthodox with discretion.

5. Finally, Scholasticism has little by little hardened certain positions of St. Thomas, thus making the dialogue with the Orthodox still more difficult.

In conclusion, Maximos IV observed: "That which is divine is infinitely rich and varied. There is nothing more impoverishing than to contemplate it from a single perspective." [3]

II

THE RECOGNITION BY THE ORTHODOX
OF THE SACRAMENTS OF OTHER CHRISTIANS

This question depends largely on the recognition by the Orthodox of the validity of the orders of other Christians. In fact,

[3] *Op. cit.*, p. 499: "Le divin est infiniment riche et varié. Rien n'est plus appauvrissant que de le contempler sous un seul angle."

only a true priest or a true bishop can, in the view of the Orthodox, administer valid sacraments, due allowance being made for
baptism.

Recently a few good works have appeared which shed new
light on the whole problem. Indeed they give grounds for hoping
that the Orthodox will find a way of adapting their ancient
canons in view of the unprecedented movement toward unity
among the Churches, an impulse that certainly derives from the
Holy Spirit. If anything is proper to Christian East, it is its adapt-
ability to God's charism. Some Orthodox authors, such as
Zander (p. 92), conclude more or less explicitly that the canons
are "of no help" in our age since their observance renders participation in the ecumenical movement impossible for the Orthodox. Afanasiev (p. 63) recognizes that "the majority of the
canonical decisions" of the ancient councils "can no longer be
applied to modern Church life in their literal sense". "The
Church demands a creative attitude toward contemporary life,"
says the same author (p. 65), and he stresses that "the doctrine
of the immutability of the canons, which we often encounter at
the present time, represents the rejection of a creative attitude
toward contemporary life".

One must, however, respect the view of those Orthodox who
do not see how the canons of the ancient ecumenical councils
can be changed without another council, the highest authority
for them. Cotsonis' works best exemplify the severity of the ancient canons in regard to the recognition of the sacraments of
heretics and schismatics. The 46th canon of the holy apostles and
the 32nd canon of Laodicea declare invalid the eucharist consecrated by heretics. The 1st canon of Carthage (also the 46th and
47th canons of the apostles) considers invalid baptism and confirmation when administered by heretics. As for marriage and
the sacrament of penance, there are no explicit canons, but
Cotsonis (p. 195, n. 35) gives a large bibliography to prove that
a marriage may be considered valid only if it had been blessed by
an Orthodox priest, and that absolution is valid only when imparted by Orthodox priests who have a special authorization
from their bishop. The sacrament of anointing is also invalid

when administered by heretics or schismatics, since they are not true priests. The holy orders of the heteredox are declared invalid by the 1st canon of Carthage and by the 45th and 47th canons of the apostles. According to the 1st canon of Carthage, says Cotsonis (p. 44), "not only is the heteredox clergyman not considered as such, but also as unbaptized". In regard to orders, however, the ancient canons are conflicting. One canon (68th of the apostles) considers invalid all orders of any heterodox, whereas three canons (19 Nicaea I; 8 Laodicea; 12 Theophilus of Alexandria) declare invalid the orders of only some heretics, and four canons (8 Nicaea I; 9 and 68 Carthage; 1 Basil) recognize the validity of the orders of others. All these canons were simultaneously confirmed by the Council in Trullo (Can. 2) and have, therefore, the same validity. Thus the Orthodox Churches do not know what attitude they should adopt today toward Catholics and Protestants, who were never defined as heretics or schismatics by the canons. Cotsonis prefers the 68th canon of the apostles because it gives a general rule, which should prevail unless something else is decided (p. 56) by individual Orthodox Churches.

This is strict adherence to the letter of the canons. By *economy,* however, orders and the other sacraments can be recognized as valid.

What precisely *economy* means was investigated recently by Thomson. His study is a fine survey of the different theories on *economy* held by Orthodox authors, and the bibliography indicated in the footnotes is virtually complete.

The theory of *economy* is based upon the principle that outside the Orthodox Church there is no grace; therefore, the sacraments of the non-Orthodox are mere external forms. For special reason, according to some Orthodox authors, however, the Church can validate these rites, miraculously reviving them by opening up the streams of grace they are supposed to convey. However, this and similar opinions are opposed by other Orthodox theologians (such as Alivisatos) who deny to the Church the power "to convert the has-not-been into the has-been", as Florovsky (p. 123) puts it. Thomson's conclusions are distressing: there is no official doctrine about *economy* among the Orthodox, no agreement of any sort among theologians; the extreme theories (what is invalid the Church can make valid) "seem to have arisen in an attempt to explain how the Church could accept or reject the validity of the same sacraments at different times, or at the same time by different autocephalous Churches" (*ibid.*, 418: in Russia, Catholic baptism was considered valid, while in Greece Catholics were rebaptized); if "what is invalid can be made valid, all the sacraments become unobligatory symbols" and "then the economy becomes *the* sacrament" (*ibid.*).

The strongest Orthodox voice against the theories of *economy* seems to be that of Florovsky: "The economical interpretation is not the teaching of the Church. It is only a private 'theological opinion', very late and very controversial, having arisen in a period of theological confusion and decadence in a hasty endeavor to disassociate Orthodox from Roman theology as sharply as possible" (p. 125; in Thomson, p. 391). It is hard to see how the decisions of various Churches about recognizing or not recognizing the validity of sacraments can be based on *economy*, when no one knows exactly what this term means. It may be hoped, however, that today's earnest search for what is common and unifying in various theological traditions will lead, through a respectful and charitable dialogue, to new ways of adapting the ancient canons to modern life, whether such adaptation be called *economy* or something else. What is important is neither canons nor *economy,* but that such adaptation be based on a new theology which recognizes that "separated Churches and Christian communities . . . are by no means deprived of significance and importance in the mystery of salvation" and are, therefore, used by the Spirit of Christ "as means of salvation which derive their efficacy from the very fullness of grace and truth entrusted to the Catholic Church" (*Decree on Ecumenism*, n. 3). One would hope that the Orthodox will adopt a similar attitude toward the Catholic Church and other Christian communities. As a matter of fact, such a mutual attitude seems to exist already; otherwise one cannot explain the very cordial relations between "sister churches", as Pope Paul VI expressed it with regard to the Catholic and the Orthodox Churches during his visit to Constantinople and at the Roman meeting with Patriarch Athenagoras I. The so-called "indirect" recognition of heterodox sacraments, which seems to Cotsonis (p. 47) to be implied in the exchange of official letters between the heads of Orthodox and non-Orthodox Churches and in forms of address like "Dear brother in Christ", can now be found in almost any document referring to the relations between Churches. These and many other signs of such recognition have rendered obsolete the severity of the ancient canons. As regards Catholic orders or sacraments in general, no Orthodox seems to doubt their validity, though some still consider Catholics as schismatics or heretics, from whose sacraments the Orthodox Church can "cut the stream of grace" (cf. the words of the Russian patriarch Sergius, cited in Thomson, p. 391) or, if they are in good faith, open it again by *economy*.

III

THE ORTHODOX ON ANGLICAN ORDERS TODAY

The validity of Anglican orders is one of the greatest ecumenical problems for both Catholics and Orthodox. The Catholic position is known and treated in any standard manual of dogmatic theology that comments on the Bull *Apostolicae curae* of 1896. The latest on this issue are the works of Francis Clark, who sustains invalidity, and Hughes (cf. *Concilium* 31) who, encouraged by the wish expressed by Cardinal Heenan to have an *ad hoc* commission composed of Catholics and Anglicans, and by the speech at Vatican Council II of Bishop Green of Port Elizabeth on December 12, 1963, attempts to reopen the question.

The Orthodox have adopted various views on the validity of Anglican orders. The ecumenical patriarch in 1922 formally proclaimed that Anglican orders "possess the same validity as those of the Roman, Old Catholic and Armenian Churches" (cf. Thomson, p. 369), without defining, however, what validity the sacraments of these Churches have. According to Cotsonis (p. 34), this recognition was made only for the case of a union between the two Churches, so that no reordination of Anglican clergymen would be necessary. It should be noted, in the light of what was said above, that even if reordination is not required in the eventuality of union, this still does not mean, for some Orthodox at least (it would, of course, for Catholics), that the orders are valid before reunion, for in the event of union they would be revivified by the Church. Be this as it may, in 1923 the Churches of Jerusalem and Cyprus followed Constantinople in recognizing Anglican orders, and in 1930 the Church of Alexandria and in 1936 the Rumanian Church did the same with certain conditions. The validity of these orders was discussed at length (cf. *Dejanija*) in a theological conference of Orthodox Churches in Moscow in 1948. During that conference a great divergence of opinions was revealed, and it was resolved at the end to postpone the whole question until the Anglican Church changes its teaching from the dogmatic, canonical and ecclesiological points of view, or, in other words, until the Anglican Church officially proclaims the Orthodox belief in sacraments.

In 1966 an inter-Orthodox commission for the dialogue with Anglicans met in Belgrade (Sept. 1-15) in virtue of a decision taken at the third Pan-Orthodox Conference at Rhodes. One of the main questions was the validity of Anglican orders. Again the divergence among the speakers was too great, and no agreement was reached. It was only declared (Archbishop Basil's Report A, p. 102) that the synodal decisions in this regard of some Churches, though valid, do not represent the official teaching of Orthodoxy and that on this account a dialogue is possible, for the time being, only through contacts with individual Churches.

A few months later, the Russians took advantage of an official meeting in London, November 10-11, 1966 (Archbishop Basil's Report B), to treat this question. The Russians had had some contacts with the Anglican Church in the last century (cf. Gill) and had produced some fine works on Anglican orders after *Apostolicae curae* in 1896. It was a recent study by Voronov, based on these works, which was discussed at the London meeting, even though the Russian delegates declared that it does not represent the official teaching of the Russian Church (Basil B, p. 204). Voronov (p. 23) arrives at the following conclusions:

1. The Anglican Church does not consider priestly ordination a sacrament, that is, a sacred action of divine institution in which the one ordained receives the special grace of the priesthood, which is not possessed in any way by a non-ordained layman. This grace is so indispensable that someone who has not received it not merely does not have the right, but does not even have the power, no matter what the circumstances, to administer the holy sacraments, with the sole exception of baptism (in cases especially provided for).

2. By denying the transformation of bread and wine into the true body and true blood of the Lord Jesus Christ, by not giving, therefore, to the eucharist the sense of an unbloody sacrifice of divine institution (especially, of a propitiatory sacrifice), the Anglican Church departs significantly from the authentic notion of the nature of the priesthood; it therefore departs as well from the intention that the Church has of possessing and of continually renewing (by ordination) "a hierarchy that is constituted of priests, one of whose main tasks and duties is the administration in the Church of the seven saving sacraments, among which the supreme sacrament is the Holy Eucharist". Thus Voronov does not see any possibility, for the time being, of recognizing Anglican orders until the Anglican Church accepts the Orthodox notions of the priesthood and the eucharist.

In the London meeting the "sacramentality" of both orders and the eucharist was to some extent defended by Anglican delegates, but it was made clear that the Anglican Church also admits the contrary opinions as legitimate. Thus the meeting failed. Indeed it is difficult to see how the Russians could recognize as priests those Anglican clergymen who themselves profess not to be such.

IV
THE CATHOLIC RECOGNITION OF ORTHODOX SACRAMENTS

Last year in *Concilium* (Vol. 28) I pleaded for a recognition of jurisdiction in the Orthodox Churches for all acts performed by their hierarchy and priests that are not contrary to Scripture, Catholic teaching or natural law. This plea was supported by texts of Vatican Council II that seem to recognize a hierarchical communion with the Orthodox Churches insofar as there exist common elements for the dispensation of the grace of God to the Christian people. In the administration of the sacraments and sacramentals (cf. Bobrinskoy), in particular, the "common elements" cover almost all aspects of the Church's life, so much so that Catholics often use the liturgical books edited by Orthodox and vice versa. The Council recognizes that the Orthodox "possess true sacraments, above all—by apostolic succession— the priesthood and the eucharist, whereby they are still joined to us in a very close relationship (*Decree on Ecumenism,* n. 15).

No serious Catholic has ever doubted the validity of Orthodox sacraments in general. They are, indeed, administered with the proper matter and form by a minister having a right intention and acting in the name of Christ. Yet for three Orthodox sacraments that require true jurisdiction some doubts about validity have existed among Catholic authors, so that it is not completely clear whether the Council's "true sacraments" embrace all seven sacraments or only some of them.

For baptism, holy orders, the eucharist and matrimony there is no difficulty; no special power in the minister is needed for the first, the *potestas ordinis* is sufficient for the second and the third, and the Orthodox are not bound to contract marriage in the form prescribed by Catholic Canon Law. The opinions of the authors are, or rather were, quite different with regard to the sacraments of penance, confirmation and the anointing of the sick. Their doubts about the validity of these sacraments, when administered by Orthodox, derive from the conviction that Orthodox bishops have no jurisdiction whatsoever since they are not in a hierarchical communion with the pope. Thus, whenever a *potestas jurisdictionis* is needed for the valid administration of sacraments, the Orthodox bishops are unable to confer it to their priests. However, authors like Coussa (pp. 25-26), Herman (p. 1053) and Jugie (ed. 1136) admitted that the absolution of Orthodox priests is valid because of a tacit concession of jurisdiction by the pope for the good of souls. They could admit no more, since all Orthodox clergy were considered, as Jugie said, to be *en bloc sous l'excommunication* and living outside the Church (p. 1136). Jugie even said that any opinion that would recognize an ordinary or delegated jurisdiction to Orthodox bishops or priests was "intolerable to the ears of theologians" (col. 1138). Now, however, the Council stresses that the Orthodox are in "a certain, though imperfect, communion with the Catholic Church" (*Decree on Ecumenism,* n. 3), and the *Ecumenical Directory* (n. 19) most clearly affirms that Can. 2314 of the *Codex iuris canonici* about excommunication for heresy or schism does not apply to those who were born in an Orthodox Church because they are not guilty of the sin of schism. Similarly unacceptable is Herman's opinion (pp. 1053-55), which asserted that Orthodox bishops are *iure divino* incapable of any ordinary jurisdiction. This opinion is unacceptable because it is based on a theology which holds that the Orthodox are totally cut off from ecclesiastical communion. Here it might be noted that even before Vatican Council II there were authors who, speaking usually on the sacrament of penance, did recognize a delegated, or even ordinary, jurisdiction in Orthodox bishops and priests (cf. Herman, pp. 1050-53). The arguments with which they supported their view, however (cf. A.B. in *L'Ami du clergé*), were too weak to remove the two chief obstacles to a serene recognition of the jurisdiction of Orthodox bishops: excommunication and the denial of all, even partial, communion between Catholics and Orthodox.

The validity of confirmation when administered by Orthodox priests is asserted to be doubtful for two reasons: first, in some

Churches the anointing is administered not *ipsa ministri manu,* as a decree of the Holy Office of June 14, 1885 insists, but by means of some instrument, which doubt the Council did nothing to remove; second, because it is believed by a great many authors that simple priests, in the quality of *ministri extraordinarii,* cannot validly administer this sacrament without a special delegated jurisdiction from the pope, or, according to others, from their bishops.

Theologians try to explain the necessity of such jurisdiction by rather divergent arguments (cf. a summary in Cappello, n. 147) which might, perhaps, be examined afresh in dialogue with the Orthodox. Orthodox authors would require no more than *potestas ordinis* in a priest for a valid administration of confirmation, although they admit that the priest acts in this as a representative of the bishop (cf. Melia 5). But such an opinion is called by Cappello (*ibid.*) erroneous and at least implicitly proscribed by the letter of Pius X of December 26, 1910.

Have Orthodox priests the supposedly necessary jurisdiction? There were theologians who denied this even for Oriental Catholic priests until Benedict XIV decided the question (cf. Deslandes). He said that the Holy See tacitly recognized this jurisdiction since, though always aware of the Oriental practice, it did not reprove, but permitted it. Did Benedict XIV recognize it also for the Orthodox? Until now the authors were divided on this point. The Holy See has usually considered the confirmation performed by the Orthodox as only probably valid, requiring a reconfirmation *secreto et sub conditione* (Herman, 1053, n. 32) in candidates for orders who were formerly Orthodox.

Also, in regard to the sacrament of the anointing of the sick some authors have had doubts as to its validity when administered by Orthodox priests. The *tutior* opinion holds that a special blessing of the holy oils is necessary for the validity of this sacrament (Cappello, Vol. III, n. 58), which blessing should be performed by a bishop or a priest having special delegation (jurisdiction). Here the same difficulty arises: on the one hand, if the Orthodox bishops have no power of jurisdiction, they cannot delegate to their priests faculties to perform the blessing of the oils; on the other hand, it is not certain that the Holy See tacitly grants faculties for it to Orthodox priests. However, since Oriental priests themselves bless the oils for each administration of the sacrament, it would follow that this sacrament would be certainly valid among the Orthodox only when administered by a bishop.

It may be hoped that after the Council no author will still have such doubts. The Council's recognition of "true sacraments" among the Orthodox, and of "a certain, though imperfect, communion with the Catholic Church", the pope's recognition of Orthodox bishops as "pastors of the portion of the flock of Christ that has been entrusted to them" [4] and his calling the Orthodox Churches "sister Churches", the permission of intercommunion under certain conditions for the eucharist, penance and the anointing of the sick, the recognition of the validity of confirmation administered by Oriental priests with no other limitation than the use of chrism blessed by a bishop, and, in general, the whole attitude of the Catholic Church to the ecumenical movement—all are proof that jurisdiction is recognized in Orthodox bishops and priests, at least to the extent that they can validly administer all seven sacraments. Indeed, the conciliar texts seem to mean much more, and they are basic for the plea mentioned at the beginning of this section.

[4] On the meeting with Athenagoras in Constantinople on July 25, 1967, cf. *L'Osservatore Romano,* July 27, 1967, p. 2, col. 6: "En se reconnaissant et en se respectant comme pasteurs de la partie du troupeau du Christ qui leur est confiée."

BIBLIOGRAPHY

I

THE NEED OF A MORE ADEQUATE SACRAMENTAL THEOLOGY

J. N. Crespel, "Parole et Sacrament," *Verbum Caro* 21 (1967), no. 83, pp. 1-27.
M. Jugie, *Theologia dogmatica christianorum orientalium ab Ecclesia*

Catholica dissidentium. De sacramentis, Vol. III (Paris, 1930); Vol. V (Paris, 1935).

W. de Vries, *Sakramententheologie bei den Nestorianern, Orientalia Christiana Analecta,* no. 133 (Rome, 1947); *Sakramententheologie bei den Syrischen Monophysiten, Orientalia Christiana Analecta,* no. 125 (Rome, 1940).

Th. Spačil, *Doctrina theologiae orientis separati de sacramentis in genere, Orientalia Christiana Analecta,* no. 113 (Rome, 1937).

J. Chrysostomus, "Ist eine *autonome* bzw. bodenständige Theologie der katholischen Orientalen notwendig und möglich?" *Una Sancta* 20 (1965), 33-42.

B. Schultze, "Catholic Theology in East and West; Uniformity or Diversity?" *Unitas* (English ed.) 16 (1964), 187-206; "Teologia latina e teologia orientale," *Problemi e orientamenti di teologia dogmatica,* Vol. I (Milan, 1957), pp. 547-579.

Maximos IV, cf. *L'Eglise Grecque Melkite au Concile* (Beyrouth, 1967), pp. 498-99.

II

THE RECOGNITION BY THE ORTHODOX
OF THE SACRAMENTS OF OTHER CHRISTIANS

L. A. Zander, *Vision and Action* (London, 1952).

N. N. Afanasiev, "The Canons of the Church: Changeable or Unchangeable," *St. Vladimir's Seminary Quarterly* II (1967), 54-58.

J. Cotsonis, "The Validity of the Anglican Orders," *The Greek Orthodox Theological Review* (Spring 1958—Summer 1958).

F. J. Thomson, "Economy. An Examination of the Various Theories of Economy Held within the Orthodox Church, with Special Reference to the Economical Recognition of the Validity of Non-Orthodox Sacraments," *The Journal of Theological Studies* 16 (1965), 368-420.

G. Florovskij, "The Limits of the Church," *Church Quarterly Review* 117 (October 1933) (as quoted in Thomson).

III

THE ORTHODOX AND ANGLICAN ORDERS TODAY

F. Clark, *Anglican Orders and Defect of Intention* (London, 1956); *Eucharistic Sacrifice and the Reformation* (London and Westmin-

ster), 1960; "Les ordinations anglicanes, problème oecuménique,"
Gregorianum 45 (1964), 60-93.

J. J. Hughes, "Two English Cardinals on Anglican Orders," *Journal
of Ecumenical Studies* 4 (1967), 1-26; "The Papal Condemnation
of Anglican Orders: 1896," *ibid.*, 235-267; *Concilium* 31 (1968).

Archbishop Basil, Report A, "La Commission Inter-Orthodoxe pour
le dialogue avec les anglicans," *Messager de l'Exarchat du Patri-
arche Russe en Europe Occidentale* 15 (1967), 74-106. Report
B: "Les entretiens théologiques concernant les ordres anglicanes
entre l'Eglise Anglicane et l'Eglise Orthodoxe Russe," *ibid.*,
201-214.

J. Gill, "The Church of England and Reunion," *Unitas* 2 (1947),
145-162; "Russian Orthodoxy and Anglicanism," *ibid.*, 6 (1951),
137-148.

L. Voronov, "La question de la hiérarchie Anglicane à la lumière
de la théologie Orthodoxe russe," *Messager de l'Exarchat du Patri-
arche Russe en Europe Occidentale,* nos. 54-55, 75-122; no. 56,
179-221; no. 57, 4-23.

IV
The Catholic Recognition of Orthodox Sacraments

I. Žužek, "Opinions on the Future Structure of Oriental Law,"
Concilium 28 (1967).

B. Bobrinskoy, "Les sacramentaux dans l'Eglise Orthodoxe," *Le
Messager Orthodoxe* 26 (1964), 50-56.

A. Coussa, *Epitome praelectionum de iure ecclesiastico orientali,* Vol.
I (Rome, 1948).

A. Herman, "Quibus legibus subiiciantur dissidentes rituum orientalium," *Il diritto ecclesiastico* 62 (1951), 1043-1058.

M. Jugie, "Pénitence dans l'Eglise Gréco-Russe," *Dictionnaire de
Théologie Catholique* XII, cols. 1127-1138.

A. B., "Le sacrement de Pénitence est-il administré validement chez
les schismatiques, dit Orthodoxes, en dehors des cas de danger de
mort?" *L'Ami du clergé* 59 (1949), 554-555.

F. M. Cappello, *Tractatus canonico moralis de sacramentis,* Vol. I
(Taurini-Romae, 1951); Vol. III, 1958.

E. Melia, "Le sacrement de confirmation," *Le Messager Orthodoxe*
8 (1959), 4-11.

J. Deslandes, "Le prêtre oriental ministre de la confirmation," *Echos
d'Orient* 29 (1930), 5-15.

PART III
DOCUMENTATION
CONCILIUM

Office of the Executive Secretary
Nijmegen, Netherlands

Concilium General Secretariat/*Nijmegen, Netherlands*

Groups of People Forgotten or Neglected in the Institutional Church

The previous articles have mainly dealt with the juridical order of elements in the Church that are preeminently sacred, namely, the sacraments. There is no doubt that when an institution like the Church turns toward the ordering of its affairs, it will begin with that field which it considers specifically its own. In the course of history, however, the Church has never limited itself to that which is sacred. It has always been in contact with other fields under the control of other authorities. It is enough to refer to the investiture struggle or the doctrinal conflicts about the teaching on the two swords or the Church's fierce opposition at the time of the Enlightenment against being reduced to a Church of the sacristy. In our own days, too, the Church is becoming conscious of the fact that it must be both a Church of worship and a Church of culture; that it has not only a purely religious contribution to make but must also cooperate in making this common world more inhabitable.

This consciousness emerged particularly during Vatican Council II and found a modest expression in Schema XIII. The question is whether this broadening of the Church's self-awareness will be reflected in the new Canon Law. When the Church addresses itself more consciously to the world and deliberately assumes a worldly function as well, it is bound to discover structures in society that differ totally from those that were prevalent when Canon Law was first formulated. There are problems today that would have been unthinkable in a closed Christian community: a juridical statute for victims of broken marriages, the right to create a revolution, the right to development, room in the legal system for an effective recognition of the rights of man, the question of the Church's juridical competence to exclude someone from the Christian community or to prevent someone from making contact with other Christians.

In view of the pastoral purpose of this documentation it is not our intention to deal with all these aspects in detail, but simply to draw attention to the new or changed status of those groups in the Church for whom there was no room or legal need in existing Canon Law because ecclesiastical and social structures made it impossible to treat these problems as juridically realistic. The mention of some forgotten groups in the Church is therefore not meant to be read as a reproach to the legislators as if they had been neglectful and had ignored them deliberately. Rather, the point is that in some cases, as in those of the poor or of those that have abandoned their sacred office, some modest attempts are already being made at a juridical integration of these groups. These attempts might conceivably have some influence on the new codification of Church law.

The fact that the juridical authority of the Church did not pay attention to some groups of Christians may also be due to other factors than changes in ecclesiastical and social structures. Like every other institution, the organization of the Church as a whole must take man primarily as he is in the normal situation. However, it is a fact that the actual Church does not consist only of such people in such a normal situation. As in every institution, there are fringe cases, people who receive no publicity because they have no specific social status. Therefore, it is not astonishing that, before they were reduced from being the "ordinary people" to "third-class citi-

zens", the laity barely received a separate mention in Canon
Law, just as they received no separate mention in the civil
code. Therefore, it seemed appropriate not to overlook this
aspect when we deal with some groups that seem to have been
forgotten in the Church.

There are groups in the Church to whom no official attention has been given because of the juridical structures of the
Church itself or because of a theological mentality that continues to operate traditionally, and there are groups that were
overlooked because a certain lack of social recognition deprived them of publicity.[1]

I

GROUPS OVERLOOKED BECAUSE OF A SITUATION CONFLICTING
WITH THE JURIDAL STRUCTURES OF THE CHURCH

1. *The Divorcees*

Apart from the question whether marriage is by nature indissoluble, it is a fact that the message of salvation sees this
indissolubility in a religious and Christian perspective. It signifies God's faithfulness to his covenant and Christ's faithfulness
to his Church. This indissolubility is an ethical requirement
and a mandate. It is obviously incorporated in the Church's
juridical order as a legal statute. Married partners may, however, fall short of this ethical requirement. Our society then
accepts the possibility of divorce. There are in fact Christian
marriages that have been dissolved in civil law. In France, for
instance, one out of every ten ecclesiastical marriages ends up
in divorce. Of every four marital cases brought before an ecclesiastical tribunal, three deal with the possibility of remarriage for at least one of the partners.[2] If not successful, these

[1] This documentation deals therefore with groups that receive not
enough if any attention from the institutional Church. It is obvious that
individual Christians, and in some cases higher authorities, are not aban-
doning these groups to their fate.

[2] "Les divorcés non rémariés et les femmes séparées," in *La Docu-*

people are juridically unable to marry again in the eyes of the Church. For these people no juridical statute exists within the institutional Church that would apply to their situation. If they wish to marry again, this is legally impossible within the Roman Catholic Church.

In Eastern Catholic law there is room for remarriage, although of course under special conditions. One cannot dispose of this by quoting the old juridical adage: *dura lex sed lex* (the law is hard but it is the law). After an appeal by divorced women, the French hierarchy published a statement on this question which struck a less harsh note than that of this harsh legislation. The bishops were sympathetic to the material, spiritual and social hardships of these divorcees. However, they do not suggest a possible change in their juridical status. Yet, they point out that these Christians understand nothing of the juridical demands of their Church, "the less so", says the text, "since many priests of this Church advise them to remarry". The bishops appeal to the Christian community to help these people by making it possible for them to lead a normal social life and by seeing to it that they do not consider themselves outcasts.

According to the statement these people are avoided by

mentation catholique, 1502 (1967), cc. 1711-6. A good bibliography on the remarriage of Catholic divorcees may be found in V. J. Pospishil, *Divorce and Remarriage—Towards a New Catholic Teaching* (New York, 1967); practical advice is given by M. Champagne, in his *Facing Life Alone* (Indianapolis, 1967); for the question of children from broken homes, see Jeanne Delais, *Le dossier des enfants du divorce* (Paris, 1967); cf. S. Lener, "Un 'libro bianco dei figli del divorzio'," in *Civiltà Catolica* 119 (Feb., 1968) 2823, pp. 241-7; for the development in theological thought about the indissolubility of marriage, see R. Araud, "Evolution de la théologie du marriage," in *Cahiers Laennec* 27,2 (June, 1967), pp. 56-71, and for a survey of Protestant theological opinion on this point, see F. Böckle, "Les problèmes du marriage interconfessionel vus sous leur aspect théologique," in IDO-C 67, 36, fol. 9-12, note 10; for the relation between civil and ecclesiastical jurisdiction with regard to divorce, see S. Lener, "Divorzio consensuale, constituzione e democrazia," in *La Civiltà Catolica,* n. 2813 (1967), c. 345-57; "Liberali divorzisti," *ibid.,* n. 2811 (1967), pp. 266-73.

their fellow Christians, and it points to some groups that have been organized in order to assist these people pastorally and socially. Therefore, a solution is indicated at the level of relief and works of mercy, which is already something. But it is obvious that a change in their legal status would be far more effective, particularly in the case of those that have been abandoned by their married partner, because their present position in the Church encourages discrimination. On the one hand, those who have been abandoned in this way should be given a social statute which provides them with greater security in modern society,[3] and on the other, the legal treatment of indissolubility and particularly the canonical status of those who are factually divorced should be studied afresh. A future volume of *Concilium* on Moral Theology will deal with these questions.

2. *Priests Married without Dispensation*

Connected with the group mentioned above are those priests who consider themselves no longer bound by the present legislation of the Church regarding celibacy. A married priest, even if married with dispensation, can no longer exercise his function, even if he wanted to; he has lost his priestly status. No sensible theologian doubts the value of the charism of celibacy as a religious vocation. The difficulty lies in that the Church has linked this charism juridically with the exercise of a specific function within the Church. A candidate for the priesthood cannot be ordained without the promise to remain unmarried. Some military and scientific institutions

[3] S. Keil, "Zur Situation des ledigen Menschen in der modernen Gesellschaft," in *Ehe* 3 (1967), pp. 97-108. There is a good survey of changing opinion with regard to indissolubility and the possibility of remarriage in A. R. Winnet, *The Church and Divorce. A Factual Survey* (London, 1968); although mainly concerned with Anglicanism, he also refers to Orthodox, Catholic and Protestant authors. The Jesuit American periodical *America* devoted four articles to the reform of Canon Law concerning marriage, annulment and divorce, in n. 17, Feb. 1968. For the views of a Catholic psychiatrist, see J. Dominian, "Vatican II and Marriage," in *The Clergy Review* (Jan. 1967), p. 26.

demand something similar of their candidates. But there, it is a matter of a temporary contract with those military or scientific institutions. In the case of the priesthood, however, Canon Law demands that this unmarried state be permanent under pain of loss of function with the result that such a priest suffers, so to speak, a social stigma and loses caste. When a priest who has accepted ordination under these conditions marries without the necessary dispensation, sometimes very difficult to obtain, his marriage is null and void, with all the legal consequences that this implies. This may lead to the same paradoxical situations that afflict the divorcees: the ecclesiastical community, or at least the legislative authority, considers him as not married with all the consequences and sanctions of that fact, while in the eyes of the civil community he is fully and validly married with all the social implications of this status.

Marc Oraison[4] has raised the question how far this situation has been influenced by a too narrow concept of the Church and how far this legislation is still dictated by the notion that the priesthood constitutes a special class. Historically it is certain that the development of celibacy as an institution shows no such thing as a straight, regular, harmonious and undisputed development. There has been frequent opposition to the *obligation* of celibacy, and it was always the danger to clerical morals which was advanced as its strongest argument.[5] Such an obligation cannot be justified by merely pointing to the inner connection between priesthood and the unmarried state. Neither the priesthood nor the unmarried state are static factors. The unmarried state depends for its value on the society in which the unmarried person lives; the priesthood depends for its value on the actual Church whose function the priest now fulfills. One of Oraison's great merits is to have pointed to the social factors that lie behind celibacy.

[4] M. Oraison, *Het celibaat. Een blijvende discussie* (Helmond, n.d. but the year is 1968).
[5] *Loc. cit.*, p. 117.

Here much will still have to happen before the situation is ripe enough for new legislation in this field.

One of the historical factors which has led to this obligation is the necessary and gradual institution of the "clergy" as a social class on its own which was able to save or rebuild a threatened civilization, a social class made up of "the clergy"; the Church became a social organization, a specific social body, based on the priesthood and priestly functions, and "socialized" as such by the force of circumstance. It is no exaggeration to maintain that in those tumultuous days the need for organizing a powerful social bulwark contributed at least implicitly to the fact that what had been understood as a spiritual ideal in a totally different context was transformed into a law of the ecclesiastical community. The present dissatisfaction with the juridical obligation to celibacy may therefore well be partly the result of our growing awareness of the Church's historicity. Now that our civilization has outgrown those antiquated features, the clergy has ceased to exist as a leading social class.

At the end of the 18th century there were still three classes in Europe, the clergy, the nobility and the "third" class which was still nondescript. The French revolution put an end to this particular partition. But the consequences of this are still far from having reached their full implications.[6] If the legal obligation of celibacy for the priest has been partly caused by the fact that the priesthood became a clerical class in this historical development of the Church, then the appropriate legislation must be revised when the priesthood is no longer such a separate class in our social and cultural situation. A legal imposition of celibacy may have been legitimate in a particular society (as in the Middle Ages); it need not be so today. In any case we shall have to think about a legal statute for the married priest.[7] Like all the other faithful the married priest,

[6] Loc. cit., p. 120.

[7] F. Wulf, "Ist das Zölibatsgesetz heute noch angebracht?" in Geist und Leben 40,4 (1967), pp. 301-6; R. Moffat, "Celibacy and Regionalism," in The Month 39,5 (1968), pp. 287-94; W. Dirks, "Gruppenbin-

too, is entitled to a legal position within the Church and he, too, has inalienable rights within the framework of the rights of man. It might be possible to think of a legal statute which allows somebody to renounce marriage temporarily without creating a permanent obligation, as is done in the military and scientific institutions mentioned above.

If married priests are mentioned here as one of the forgotten groups in the Church, this refers principally to their juridical status. In regard to pastoral treatment there already exist such bodies as the Dutch CAPER (Central Advice Bureau for Priests and Religious) or the American NAPR (the National Association for Pastoral Renewal), and there is a similar body in France. For effectiveness, however, they need the cooperation of the ecclesiastical authorities which they cannot rely on in all countries. Assistance could be far more effective if this group of Christians were given a legal position. It is indeed obvious that there is more to this problem than the juridical aspect. The other aspects have been barely mentioned here because the next pastoral issue of *Concilium* will deal with them.

II

GROUPS OF PEOPLE FORGOTTEN BECAUSE OF A THEOLOGICAL MENTALITY
IN THE CHURCH: THE SCIENTISTS

These people receive too little attention not primarily because of the ecclesiastical and juridical structures of the Church but because of a peculiar theological mentality which will, of course, indirectly penetrate the structures. The exact sciences have had to wage a fierce battle before their emanci-

dungen der Zölibatäre," in *Frankfurter Hefte* 23,3 (Feb. 1968), pp. 83-7; D. Born, "Celibacy and One's Inalienable Rights," in *The Nat. Cath. Reporter* 4,19 (March 1968), p. 4; A. Antweiler, *Zur Problematik des Pflichtszölibats der Weltpriester* (Münster, 1968, pro ms.); G. Hamburger (Pseudonym), *Katholische Priesterehe oder der Tod eines Tabus?* (Hamburg, 1968).

pation from theological and philosophical supervision became a fact. But even after this emancipation a certain alienation has persisted between the official mentality of the Church and that of the scientists, in spite of all the apologetic writings about the peaceful coexistence between faith and science.[8] It is difficult to avoid a certain shudder of suspicion when ecclesiastical authorities are faced with the achievements of psychoanalysis (as applied, for instance, to the examination of candidates for the priesthood or religious life), medical science (as with the pill), sociology or physics.

There will always be a kind of healthy competition between the sciences of the mind and the exact sciences, but the Church would nevertheless lose something of its catholicity if only the sciences of the mind would feel at home in the Church. Gusdorf[9] sees the contrast between faith and science, which led to a public and significant conflict for the first time in the 17th century, against the background of the loss of a coherent life which resulted from modern developments. Both Christianity and science tend toward totalitarianism, each in its own way. In the last half-century science has learned that there is no knowledge without presupposition; it is a deductive system, built by man on the basis of various hypotheses, without ontological significance, but sure of the applause that follows success. It is precisely this success which leads an outsider easily to overrate science, and many a scientist is at present far from happy with this. There are indeed many Christians

[8] Cf. "Prophets in the Secular City" in *Concilium* 7 (1968); M. Jeuken, "Een manco van onze theologie," in *Streven* 21,8 (May 1968), pp. 780-4; D. Galtier, *Peut-on évangéliser les techniciens?* (Paris, 1966); H. Dürrbeck, "Die Verantwortung des Technikers in die hochtechnisierten Welt," in *Frankfurter Hefte* 10 (1967), pp. 683-93; D. Dubarle, *Approches d'une théologie de la Science* (Paris, 1967).

[9] G. Gusdorf, *Science et Foi au milieu du XXe siècle. Un débat de conscience de l'occidental moderne* (Paris, 1956); A. Koyre, *Du monde clos à l'univers infini* (Paris, 1962); *idem, Newtonian Studies* (Cambridge, Mass., 1965). A striking example of a scientist's approach to a point of faith may be found in J. M. de Jong, "De opstanding van Christus," in *Geloof en Natuurwetenschap* II (The Hague, 1967), pp. 67-117. For this whole problem see P. van der Hoeven, "Kroniek: mens en natuurwetenschap," in *Wending* 22,7 (Sept. 1967), pp. 389-411.

among the scientists who turn only too willingly to the faith in order to listen to another "version" of the reality in a language they can understand. Faith and science are each concerned with different aspects of this reality. Faith is a "second reading" of the reality which does not contradict the "first reading" (the scientific one). But this must show in the room the Church must make for both. Faith withdraws from the norms of universally valid objectivity: the believer can manifest the received grace, not prove it. He is led by God but his faith remains a gamble: certainty is won through danger. Science does not know this vital heart of existence, but as a human being the scientist is in need of it.

With regard to Vatican Council II there have already been complaints that an exclusive representation by bishops and theologians was too one-sided: there were no pastoral theologians, few if any sociologists, while the exact sciences were barely heard either to question or to reply. This gave scientists the impression that the Church merely existed for theologians and philosophers and that the exact sciences had nothing to do with it. But this group of Christians with the mentality of scientists is constantly on the increase. In Holland, for instance, 60 percent of the students are being trained in the exact sciences. This creates a special problem, not so much for the people but rather for the Church itself which, if it really means to be truly "catholic", has to provide a living space where these people can integrate their scientific mentality in that of their faith.

Jeuken has pointed out, for instance, that the present Dutch catechism represents only one aspect of contemporary thought and it is precisely the scientists that miss there their modern way of thinking. The juridical organization may possibly have something to contribute here when it will be involved in the new regulations about the scientific formation of future priests. No doubt, even in social life, the scientist likes to keep away from political and economic life and will therefore not be inclined to mix in Church politics and Church economics. The Church will, however, have to make every effort to involve them in the future organization of the Church and certainly let itself be informed so as not to be taken by surprise when those changes take place in the scientific world.[10] The Church would fail in its catholicity if what Cardonnel wrote were true: that, since Vatican II, it remains possible, with a great effort, to remain a Christian, but it is practically impossible to become one.[11]

III
GROUPS OF PEOPLE WHO, FOR LACK OF SOCIAL RECOGNITION, ARE NOT RECEIVING THE NECESSARY PUBLICITY

There are people who are never in the public eye whether in Church or in society at large because they are not fully socially recognized with regard to their person or their situation, and, consequently, their chances of normal and active participation in civil or ecclesiastical life are diminished. This lack of social recognition, which means for some groups a lowering of social status, being socially "written off", is not always explicit and conscious in Church or society but lies hidden in factual relationships.

1. *The Sick*

The progress in medicine has created numerous and important social, political and economic problems.[12] Until this modern age, medical science dealt practically only with acute and brief illnesses, and nursing, mainly, with incurables. Today

[10] J. C. M. Wellen, "Panorama van onze toekomst," in *Dux* 44,1 (Jan. 1968), p. 22: "The scientist is therefore highly specialized, which makes him still more isolated. This isolation is reinforced by the fact that scientific discoveries are not directly socially relevant."

[11] J. Cardonnel, "Dieu et l'urgence des masses," in *Esprit* 36, 370 (April, 1968), p. 670.

[12] R. Dubos, "La science et la nature de l'homme," in *Chronique sociale de France* (1967), 2, *Le prix du progrès,* pp. 69 and 75.

it is constantly faced with illnesses of long duration which lead to a formation of communities in hospitals which have their own rights and no longer depend on the initiative of charitable institutions or the pity of others. While formerly one suspected an element of guilt in the patient and looked on illness as a punishment, today we have a scientific investigation of the causes, and these causes are fought with increasing success, so that in this field we have experienced a complete desacralization. The sick person is neither spiritually branded nor privileged. In the Middle Ages special value was attached to a sick person's prayer. In the hospices for the sick in Palestine and the "Hôtels-Dieu" of France and other countries that took part in the crusades, representatives of the Order of St. John of Jerusalem used to appear in the evening and loudly proclaim to the sick what was expected of them: "Sick Sirs, pray for peace" (*Seigneurs malades, priez pour la paix*). This showed the responsibility of those that were ill and the expectations of those that were healthy.[13] The Church took charge of the nursing and administered the sacrament of the sick. Out of these individual sick persons there slowly developed a whole world of sick persons who saw their existence in a productive society as futile and felt themselves isolated and ignored by society. They look on themselves as people who are entitled to health.[14] For their illness they expect of the Church not merely a repetition of the dogma of original sin but rather an appeal to human solidarity and the Church's collectivity in creating goodness. They want the Church to make clear that they still "belong."

Gradually, the sick had gained a legal position which has

[13] H. Péquinot, "Les malades d'hier et d'aujourd'hui," in *Lumière et Vie* 17,86 (Jan.-Feb. 1968), pp. 3-24; Y. Congar, "Pour un bon usage de la maladie," in *A mes Frères* (= Foi vivante 71, Paris, 1968), pp. 149-62.

[14] G. Brochu, "La maladie, pourquoi?" in *Christus* 15,57 (Jan. 1968), pp. 123-9; *Kirche in der Stadt* II (Vienna, Freiburg, Basle, 1968), pp. 114-20; R. Picker, "Die Krankensalbung; Le droit à la santé—mythe ou réalité" (*Cahier Laennec* 27,1, March 1967).

led from charity to assistance, from assistance to insurance, from the duty of those that can help to the right of those that need help. In spite of these gains the sick person of today feels himself threatened by anonymity, by the prior interest shown to the illness rather than to his person, and by the way in which society expects him to put unconditional trust in medical science. Outwardly he must also submit to an administration which determines the rights and the duties of the sick person. Over against those that are healthy, he feels himself inferior, hampered in his freedom of movement, dependent on others or even frustrated in his right to good health. He expects the Church to defend his right to human and humane treatment, to care for him personally and pastorally, and to provide him with a liturgy which convinces him that he, too, belongs to the People of God on the way. For all the democratization of health services the minority, constituted by those that are ill, will always need this support, otherwise the universal right to effective care for all becomes an illusion.

2. *The Aged*

Formerly old age was itself seen as an illness (*senectus ipsa morbus*), but today the aged constitute their own social group which has been described with the word "withdrawal" (*distanciëring*) by Buytendijk.[15] Society rejects the aged but often the aged themselves begin by dropping many social connections.[16] This process embraces many different factors of which perhaps the most striking is that there is no longer room for the aged in the family. As a social institution the family has practically disappeared, and this family, which is usually a

[15] F. J. J. Buytendijk, *Algemene theorie der menselijke houding en beweging* (Utrecht, 1948), p. 510; E. Cumming, "Further Thoughts on the Theory of Disengagement," in *International Social Science Journal* XV,3 (1963), p. 3717; *La Vieillesse, problème d'aujourd'hui* (= Convergences, Paris, 1967), p. 63; G. Butty, "L'intégration du troisième âge," in *Choisir* 98,8 (Dec. 1967), pp. 8-11.
[16] J. M. A. Munnichs, "Het einde," in *Leven en eindigheid* (= Mens en Medemens, Utrecht, 1965).

second generation family, concentrates more and more on its basic functions where people no longer rely on the much lauded wisdom of the aged. But when the environment makes no demands on the aged, these old people will not do anything any more and will age even more quickly than is necessary.

In modern society youthfulness is highly rated, and this holds also for the Church. This factor explains perhaps partly the criticism of the old age of the principal officials in the Church, and it is certainly noticeable in the liturgical reform, the doctrinal development and the frank attitudes toward what were considered unshakable certainties in the past. For many old people the development is too fast. They feel that in religion, too, they are not wanted because they are no longer brought into it. Biological aging is inevitable even though medical science manages to postpone it; social aging, however, is not inevitable. Science is making valiant efforts to penetrate into this "third age" (*le troisième âge*), particularly in sociology and psychology, but a pastoral treatment of old age still seems beyond our reach.[17]

Not only medical gerontology but also social and psychological gerontology are making great strides forward. Scientists try to meet the challenge created by the new situation of this growing and widening sector of the population. The Churches cannot afford to lag behind. Old people must be drawn into an ecclesiastical social life where they feel that they are wanted. The question is not solved by merely institutionalizing the care of the aged. There must be an understanding of the changed status of old people. If in the past there was much talk about gratefulness to, and respect for, old people, today we should realize the sober fact that in the past there were fewer old people and that it is easier to feel grateful and respectful toward a small group than a constantly growing

[17] J. Eger, "Gebet und Gottesdienst im Altenheim," in *Lebendige Seelsorge* 19,2 (March 1968), pp. 86-8; J. H. Huijts, "Aspiraties van de oude dag," in *De derde levensfase* (= Geestelijke Volksgezondheid 31, Utrecht, 1966), p. 44.

group which the middle-aged see as a threat to the welfare state and the young find it hard to appreciate for their experience and wisdom, partly because these old people no longer fulfill the functions which grandparents had in the past.[18] This makes it difficult to accept old people as social partners in their own right. The attitude of society has been known to be described as contempt tempered by pity. The old person expects neither contempt nor pity of the pastor. He wants to keep in touch with us and to be involved in what is happening in the Church. He feels it as an injustice if his usefulness is judged exclusively by his productivity or measured exclusively by the standards of an age group which has all the advantages in our culture. Schreuder once said: "The *conditio sine qua non* of a positive attitude toward old people is that we learn to recognize our own fears of the vulnerability of old age and of death." [19]

Our attitude toward the aged is frequently a reaction prompted by the projection of our own fears. But this vulnerability of old age has a positive function, because it is not a casual defect of old age; it is an essential part of existence. The old person is vulnerable because in many ways he can no longer adjust himself and can no longer manage his own life. This is a basic law of the human condition. In principle no man can manage, "save" himself. It is not only a prerogative of the Christian to recognize and accept this, but also to see it within the context of the dominion of God who made our human impotence his own. Society always gains by concerning itself with a forgotten group. It then opens up a new way of "being human" and builds up its solidarity. And this is true

---

[18] R. Albrecht, *Aging in a Changing Society* (Gamesville, 1968); A. L. Vischer, *Seelische Wndlungen beim alternden Menschen* (2nd ed., Basle/ Stuttgart, 1961).
[19] J. C. Schreuder, "De ouderdom als uitdaging," in *De derde levensfase* (see n. 17), p. 35; B. Dreher, "Pastorale Grundsätze zur Altenseelsorge," in *Lebendige Seelsorge* 19,2 (March, 1968), pp. 69-73; W. Klemp, "Altenseelsorge," in *Kirche in der Stadt* II (Vienna, Freiburg, Basle, 1968), pp. 199-203.

also in the Church. The Church need not fear here that it is taking over work better done by others. Although much has been done by the Church, more is expected. Experts have pointed out that the training for geriatrics, behind which there used to lie so many vested interests, has so far been left to amateurs and public authorities because so little was done by particular initiative. It is good that the Churches have made a generous effort in this field.

3. The Unmarried

A careful analysis of Sunday sermons shows that the audience is usually supposed to be either young people or married people. Yet, the parish no longer consists merely of families: the unmarried adult forms already a large percentage of society, and therefore also of the parishioners. To illustrate this with a few figures: of the 58.3 million inhabitants of West Germany on December 31, 1963 only 28.4 million were married, the other 29.9 million were not, and so there were 1.5 million more people who were not married. There were 4.2 million who were over 25 (the average age for marriage) and who were not married. To this must be added 4.8 million of those who were no longer married.

These figures show that the unmarried state, for whatever reason, is the factual situation for a large number of people, apart from priests and religious.[20] Yet, the educational ethic in both Church and State (again apart from training institutes for priests or religious) makes it appear as if the sole aim of education is marriage. The actual situation has been different for some time already. The unmarried form a very important part of the community, a part that is clearly visible in society and simply cannot be described as a group of "left-overs", or people in whom something is missing. Our modern pluralistic society has many valuable functions for a man and a woman

[20] S. Keil, "Zur Situation des ledigen Menschen in der modernen Gesellschaft," in *Ehe* 4,3 (1967), pp. 98-9.

other than being father and mother. Karl Barth has already spoken of a decentralization of marriage.[21] Here, too, the Churches are expected to have something to say about, e.g., the sexual ethics of the unmarried man or woman. We can no longer pretend that there is only one form of sexual ethic, the ethic of marriage. On the other hand, the Churches will have to recognize the fact that the unmarried state is also a fully valid state of life for the laity. At the social level this group still has to fight discrimination (e.g., in taxes and housing); it is only right that this growing social group should expect the Churches to make a positive contribution in this field.[22]

4. *Ex-Priests and Ex-Religious*

Linked with the problem of the married priest, particularly when living in conflict with the legal structures of the Church (I,2), is the question of those priests and religious who have left with full dispensation. The lack of concern on the part of the Church has occasionally caused profound human suffering and has had far-reaching consequences with regard to normal life in society.

It is curious that people who have served the Church devotedly, sometimes for ten or twenty years, have, on their return to the world, been pushed into a situation of silence and anonymity in the Church in spite of the fact that the Church itself has regularized and therefore accepted their situation. There is perhaps no other group in the Church that feels itself so negatively and so adversely treated as these Christians.[23] Their number is no doubt relatively small but difficult to assess. It is the exception when a study of priestly vocations devotes some thought to the tragedy which may be caused by leaving the priesthood. There are nowhere exact figures of the total num-

[21] K. Barth, *Kirchliche Dogmatik* III,4 (Zürich, 1951), p. 155.

[22] J. Scharfenberg, "Ehe und Ehelosigkeit," in *Junge Gemeinde* (Jan. 1967), p. 31; C. Duquoc, "Le marriage aujourd'hui," in *Lumière et Vie* 82 (1967), pp. 33-62.

[23] Cf. *Crisis van het ambt. Visies en verwachtingen van uitgetreden priesters* (Hilversum, 1967; soon to appear in German, English and Spanish).

ber of priests and religious (male and female) who have changed their way of life.[24] One cannot escape the impression that the official ecclesiastical authorities, apart from a few exceptions, avoid giving the People of God clear information on this point. This is doubtless one, if not the main, reason why a group, estimated by some to make up 10 percent of the present number of priests and religious, has suffered such neglect, both pastorally and juridically, on the part of the Church in most countries. Gradually many of the faithful begin to realize that those who abandon their office or leave their monastery are not necessarily disloyal or lacking in a sense of duty, nor the least intelligent or the least committed members of the clergy or a religious order. Too often these people are indiscriminately ranged with the immature and the failures, and said to have abandoned their religious ideals for the sake of marriage or because they lacked discipline and religious commitment. Fortunately we no longer talk about "apostasy" here and there is a growing realization that these Christians are not only entitled to the inalienable right to the full and human attention and care of the community and the authorities but also to the opportunity to make positive contribution to the Church's pastoral mission because of their training and their pastoral experience.

One of the prerogatives the Church has always claimed is its catholicity, its universality. This can be understood geographically and then it would be enough for the Church to be

[24] For some countries the exact figures of the decline in numbers among the clergy begin to become available. A survey covering the whole Church is being prepared by Pro Mundi Vita (Brussels) in a so-called confidential note which will appear later this year. In New York, Dennis Barry is working on an investigation about 300 ex-priests, the results of which will be published by Sheed & Ward in the spring of 1969. He agrees with the well-known sociologist, Fr. J. Fichter, S.J., of Harvard University, that only the official ecclesiastical authorities can say how many priests have left during the last years. Cf. The *Nat. Cath. Reporter* of April 3, 1968, pp. 1 and 8, also reproduced in *Search* (June 1968), p. 71, which also gives some impression of the difficulties of communication on this point. But even the official annual figures would only give a limited understanding of the real dimensions of this group that we have discussed here.

present throughout the world with its Gospel. It can also be understood ethically, and then it would be enough for the Church to offer its teaching and practice as acceptable to all races without any discrimination of color or culture. It can also be understood socially, and then it means that the Church may in no sense be a Church of an élite but must stand open to every social condition. This catholicity, at its various levels, can be understood qualitatively, and then it requires a pastoral pluralism which has certainly not yet been reached. Our time demands particularly a qualitative catholicity at the anthropological level; the Church must take its message to every level of the human condition. And it knows that. A monolithic Church in the process of becoming a decentralized institute can clearly not give equal attention to all those new groups in a quickly changing society. Perhaps it still lacks the necessary structures for such a complicated task. But a renewed Church order cannot totally neglect these apparently forgotten groups. Hence it appeals for its juridical problems more than ever to sociology and other human sciences in order to avoid that the codification of its new Canon Law should already be a failure before it starts.

BIOGRAPHICAL NOTES

Tomás Garcia Barberena: Born in Spain in 1911, he was ordained in 1935. He studied at the universities of Comillas and Salamanca in Spain, and at the Lateran University in Italy. He is a doctor of Canon Law and rector of the University of Salamanca. His publications include *Commentaires au Code de droit canonique* IV (Madrid, 1964), and he is a contributor to *Revista Española de Derecho Canónico*.

Otto Ter Reegen, S.S.S.: Born in 1924 in the Netherlands, he was ordained in 1950. He studied at the Gregorian in Rome, and in the Netherlands at the universities of Utrecht and Nijmegen. With degrees in theology and Canon Law, he is a member of the Dutch Pastoral Institute, and the secretary of the Dutch Pastoral Council. His publications include "Zielzorg bij maatschappelijk bedreigden," an article written jointly with H. van Venrooy, O.P., in *Sanctissima Eucharistia* (1965-66).

Antonio Mostaza Rodríguez: Born in 1912 in Spain, he was ordained in 1937. He studied in Rome at the Gregorian, and in Spain at the universities of Comillas, Santiago de Compostela and Madrid, receiving doctorates in theology, civil and Canon Law. He is professor of Canon Law at the Faculty of Law at Valencia University. His publications include *El problema del ministro extraordinario de la confirmación* (Salamanca, 1952). He is a frequent contributor to *Revista Española de Teología* and *Revista Española de Derecho Canónico*.

Eliseo Ruffini: Born in 1924 in Italy, he was ordained in 1947. He studied at the major seminary, Como, and in the Theological Faculty of Milan University, receiving his doctorate in theology in 1960. He is a member of the Institute of Religious Studies at Fazzada, professor of dogma at the major seminary, Como, and professor of sacramental theology at Milan University. His publications include *La dottrina teologica del "sacramentum legis naturae" in S. Bernardo e Ugo di S. Vittore* (Varese, 1964).

Petrus Huizing, S.J.: Born in 1911 in the Netherlands, he was ordained in 1942. He studied at the universities of Amsterdam, Nijmegen, Louvain, Munich and the Gregorian. He holds degrees in philosophy and theology, and doctorates in both civil and Canon Law. He has held the post of professor of Canon Law and of the history of Canon Law at the University of Nijmegen since 1965. He is also adviser to the Commission for the revision of the Code of Canon Law in Rome, and is president of the "Werkgenootschap voor kanoniek recht". His publications include *La forme matrimoniale tridentine* (Hilversum-Anvers, 1966). He is a frequent contributor to *Gregorianum*.

182   BIOGRAPHICAL NOTES

1962) was *La formation de l'Église dans les Etats Unis d'Amerique a travers l'activité synodale, ave une attention particulière au probleme de* lications include *Open to the Spirit: Religious Life after Vatican II* LADISLAS ÖRSY, S.J.: Born in 1921 in Hungary, he was ordained in 1951. He studied at the Gregorian and at Oxford, obtaining degrees in philosophy, theology and Canon Law. He is professor of Canon Law in the department of theology at Fordham University, New York. His pub-

(Washington, D.C., 1968).

RINALDO FALSINI, O.F.M.: Born in 1924 in Italy, he was ordained in 1948. He studied at the Antonianum in Rome and in Paris at the Liturgical Institute. Holding degrees in theology and liturgy, he is professor of dogmatic and moral theology at the Catholic University of Milan, and an adviser to the Sacred Congregation of Rites. His publications include *La nouvelle liturgie de la Messe* (Milan, 1965). He is co-editor of *Revista Pastorale Liturgica.*

TEODORO JIMÉNEZ URRESTI: Born in 1924 in Spain, he was ordained in 1949. He studied at the Gregorian and Lateran universities in Rome, holding degrees in theology, Canon and Roman Law. He has been professor of dogma in Bilbao since 1956, and is also pro-vicar general and director of the clergy house of studies in Bilbao. His publications include *Binomio "Primado-Episcopado"* (Madrid, 1962).

EUGENIO CORECCO: Born in Switzerland in 1931, he was ordained in 1955. He studied at the Gregorian, and at the universities of Munich and Fribourg. He holds a licentiate in theology and civil law and a doctorate in Canon Law (1962), and since 1967 he has worked at the *l'administration des biens ecclesiastiques.* He is a frequent contributor to Canonical Institute of Munich University. The subject of his thesis (in *La Scuola Cattolica.*

FERDINAND KLOSTERMANN: Born in 1907 in Salzburg, he was ordained in 1929. He studied in Austria at the major seminary of Linz, and in the theological faculty of the University of Graz, receiving his doctorate in theology in 1936. He has been professor of pastoral theology in the faculty of Catholic theology of Vienna University since 1962, and is assistant-general of Austrian Catholic Action. His publications include *Prinzip-Gemeinde* (Vienna, 1965). He is a frequent contributor to the review *Der Seelsorger.*

KARL GASTGEBER: Born in 1920 in Austria, he was ordained in 1951. He studied at the universities of Graz in Austria and Tübingen in Germany, gaining doctorates in medicine and theology. He is professor of pastoral theology at the University of Graz and director of that university's Institute of Pastoral Theology. His publications include *La parole de Dieu à travers la parole de l'Homme. J.M. Sailer comme rénovateur de la prédication* (Vienna, 1964).

JOSEF HORNEF: Born in 1896 in Germany, he is a Catholic. He studied in Germany at Freiburg-im-Breisgau, Bonn and Giessen, receiving doctorates in law and Canon Law. His publications include *The New Vocation* (Cork, 1962).

IVAN ŽUŽEK, S.J.: Born in 1924 in Yugoslavia, he was ordained in 1955. He studied in Rome at the Gregorian and at the Oriental Institute. He holds degrees in theology and Canon Law, and is professor of both Canon Law and the Russian language at the Oriental Institute in Rome. His publications include *Kormcaja kniga. Studies in the Principal Code of Russian Canon Law* (1964).

International Publishers of CONCILIUM

ENGLISH EDITION
Paulist Press
Glen Rock, N. J., U.S.A.

Burns & Oates Ltd.
25 Ashley Place
London, S.W.1

DUTCH EDITION
Uitgeverij Paul Brand, N. V.
Hilversum, Netherlands

FRENCH EDITION
Maison Mame
Tours/Paris, France

JAPANESE EDITION (PARTIAL)
Nansôsha
Tokyo, Japan

GERMAN EDITION
Verlagsanstalt Benziger & Co., A.G.
Einsiedeln, Switzerland

Matthias Grunewald-Verlag
Mainz, W. Germany

SPANISH EDITION
Ediciones Guadarrama
Madrid, Spain

PORTUGUESE EDITION
Livraria Morais Editora, Ltda.
Lisbon, Portugal

ITALIAN EDITION
Editrice Queriniana
Brescia, Italy